Frances Regina Thrasher Norge

Stories of a Redneck's Wife

Dedicated to my Redneck Husband Jasen and Redneck in Training Juni.

You are the light at the end of my dark tunnel.

Chapter One: It's Just the Beginning

I told you so. Such simple words. Yet four powerful, argument-winning gems for every wife. The use of brain over brawn. A victory. Satisfaction.

Especially when the first "I told you so" comes within 24 hours of reciting your vows. A triplet of I told you so's, if you will. A beautiful thing.

We check into our hotel in Turks and Caicos. It's breathtakingly stunning. White beaches. Clear water. A suite. Perfection.

My new husband and I decided to kick off our week-long honeymoon with a walk along the beach.

"Don't forget to put on sunscreen, honey. The sun is much stronger here than at home. You should seriously put some on your feet, too. You're always wearing shoes."

"I've lived my whole life in the sun. I'm an outdoors man. I never burn."

"Okay."

I grab my new digital camera, un-sun screened husband, and

we head to the beach.

"Stay here, babe. I want to get a few pictures of you on the shore."

"Ummm…you know, I think the tide is coming in. Maybe it's not such a good idea to go out so far. That camera can't get wet."

"Don't worry, baby! I got …" Splash. The camera is sprayed with salt water. "Fuck."

"I told you so. Damn it, honey, I just bought that camera."

"Don't start with me. Once it dries, it'll be fine."

"No, it won't. it's a digital camera. Not a Polaroid from 1982. They're sensitive. We need to buy some disposable cameras."

"Hell no. I aint spending no money on some cheap-assed cameras when we have a perfectly good one right here."

Two hours pass, and the camera dries. And refuses to turn on. Dead as a door know.

"Fuck! "

"Uh huh. I told you so."

"Why the fuck would they make a camera that can't get a little water on it?"

"Because it's a professional camera. Professionals don't go

bounding into the ocean. You, on the other hand, do."

The next morning, I wake up to my husband attempting to force is swollen, fire-red, blistered feet into shoes.

"Fuck! What the fuck! I burned the tops of my fucking feet. I can't even wear shoes. Damn it!"

"I told you so."

Three waterproof cameras and a pair of flip flops later and we're on our way too…what, marital bliss? Doesn't exist. Happily ever after? Sure, if my marriage were set in a Disney Fairytale. But there are no fairy tales. Marriage is work.

My husband and I love hard and fight hard. We met like a fairy tale. But beyond that, it's a balancing act between two polar opposites.

My husband, you see, is a redneck.

Merriman-Webster defines redneck as "a white person who lives in a small town or in the country especially in the southern U.S., who typically has a working-class job, and who is seen by others as being uneducated and having opinions and attitudes that are offensive."

Wikipedia: "A derogatory slang term used in reference to poor, uneducated white farmers, especially from the southern United States. It is similar in meaning to cracker, hillbilly and white trash. I recent decades, the term has expanded its meaning to refer to bigoted, loutish reactionaries who are opposed to modern ways, and has often been used to attack white Southern conservatives. The term is used broadly to degrade working class and rural whites that are perceived by urban progressives to be insufficiently liberal. At the same time, some Southern whites have reclaimed the word, using it with pride and defiance as a self-identifier."

Okay. I thought the word redneck meant more of a literal definition. My husband's neck is literally red. From working in the sun in lieu of an office. Perhaps I would have thought twice about calling him a redneck almost hourly if I'd known the true nature of the word.

This entire book is my definition of a redneck. For one, my husband literally has a red neck. It's from working on tractors, laboring in the sun, and never lounging at the beach.

At the same time, he built our home. With cash. We own our business. We don't live in a trailer and my husband is a mathematical genius.

Can you calculate acreage in your head? Neither can I. But he can.

His political views are ridiculously conservative, I'll give the dictionaries that one. He's more than stubborn. He's downright bullheaded. It's a bitch to deal with. But he's also hilarious without intention.

He is a redneck. I am not. Makes for a ridiculously difficult, if not hilarious, life.

Even our upbringings are opposites. I tell him he has the opinions of an 80-year-old. That would stem from him living most of his formative years with his grandparents.

Jasen grew up banding cow balls. I did not. He grew up slicing piglet testicles and feeding them to the dogs. Again, I did not. He grew up eating green steaks. I absolutely did not.

Those basic differences make cooking difficult, but I let him handle any kind of slaughter, burying, and de-balling of all animals.

We live on 25 acres on the outskirts of suburbia. We live with two dogs, 10-20 cows, 2 sows, ducks, geese, and chickens.

Until I married my husband, I had visions of a city life. A

high-paced career. Clothes requiring heels. My vision changed the moment I said "I do."

I stay at home with my son and run the paperwork side of our business. My master's degree has netted me exactly $0. I wear muck boots. And I love it. I do get out into the academic world as an adjunct English professor at the local community college. No, it's not the New York Times, but I enjoy the challenge.

Life with a redneck is not easy. We fight hard and we love hard. In between, we laugh. A lot.

The First Date

My husband and I originally dated in high school. He was my first real boyfriend. My dad took one look at him and handed me a five-dollar bill "just in case you need a taxi." By the end of the summer I had a wad of five-dollar bills stuffed in my purse.

The first time he picked me up in his 1973 white-with-blue-interior 220D Mercedes I felt smitten. I loved him and that car at first sight. It smelled like vanilla sex wax. With maybe a hint of beer. Young redneck took me to a nice restaurant. He ate like he'd grown up with 12 older brothers, guarding his food like a pit bull. I was half-way through picking at my food when he sat back, grabbed his non-existent belly, and let out the loudest belch I'd ever heard.

It's important to note a little tidbit about my upbringing at this point. I took manners classes. We're talking enough silverware to make you dizzy, walking with a book on your head, and learning the exact way to cross your ankles and let your server know you're finished with the salad plate. Insanity. But educational.

So imagine my surprise when my date, the boy I'd stared at for years, burped, and then smiled "Sorry. Had to make room for more." He then took my plate, and scarfed it down. Nice.

Before we left, Jasen began eyeing the leftover bread in the center of the table. "Hey. Put these in your purse."

Who IS this guy? "Are you kidding me? You must be kidding me. Absolutely not!" I remember the tingling heat on my cheeks. The urge to run away. To use that five-dollar bill.

Apparently Jasen didn't need my purse. His pants would suffice. He stuffed countless rolls down his Ralph Laurens, left some cash on the table, and hobbled to the door. Lovely.

It was chilly that night, and par for the course his car wouldn't start. He was the first person I knew to have a cell phone. That sucker was so big it pulled the back of his pants down. But he refused to call my dad.

"It's no problem. Listen...I'm going to spray some ether under the hood. You hold this button until the car starts." Excellent. We're going to blow ourselves up, right here in the parking lot. And I'm freezing in a skirt.

Apparently, I didn't know when to let my finger off of the button. He yelled at me. My dream boy friggin yelled at me! After that night I realized no one is perfect. Even the boy I stared at. He wasn't perfect. Best date ever.

The True Beginning

"Holy shit...your tits are HUGE." Those were the first words my husband said to me after a nine-year hiatus. He's not romantic. Obviously. He is a redneck. He's a great husband, a wonderful father, an amazing provider and a slew of other gushy things. But when it comes down to it, my husband is a redneck.

We first dated in high school. I was naive, he a man-whore. Okay. Maybe that's an overstatement, but looking at him through virgin eyes, that's what I saw.

We dated for a few months, he moved on, and my eyes were no longer peering through virginal glasses. Our relationship was more off than on for the next few years. I know every one of his ex-girlfriends. That's a blessing and a curse.

After graduation I went to Virginia Tech, and he went to work. And that was it. Occasional sightings, or rocks thrown at my apartment window at 3 a.m. from him partying with his high school buddies working hard to drink themselves out of scholarships. I saw him a handful of times, but thought of him often.

I don't really know why. Our first date left me completely embarrassed. It was the late 1990s, so I'll forgive the three-sizes-too-large pants. But not asking for a to go box is ridiculous. But he made me laugh. He was the boy every girl wanted. And he got every girl he wanted.

Nine years passed. I moved on. Actually, I moved to Greensboro, NC for graduate school. I was in a semi-serious long-distant relationship when the phone rang.

It didn't take 10 seconds to know who was on the other end of the phone. It took even less than 10 seconds for my face to flush, my stomach to churn, and my brain to stop working like an educated woman's should.

He still left me stumbling over my words. He remembered my childhood phone number, talked to my dad, and called me. He said he didn't know why. He also said he wanted to "catch up sometime."

A few weeks passed, and I drove home to spend Valentine's Day with my newly-divorced dad. My parents were married for 29 years, and he was not taking the divorce well. My sister and I met my future Redneck Husband at a hockey game.

He ran up to me, covered in and literally smelling like, dirt. I'm not talking a little stain on his pants. This man was dirty. Homeless person dirty. His facial hair needed some serious attention. His head hair was down to his shoulders, and he reeked of hard liquor. His once boyish figure was too skinny for a man in his early 20s. I knew he was in a very, very bad place.

After he greeted me by complimenting my voluptuous figure, I got the hell out of that hockey game as fast as possible. This guy had some serious issues. My life was on track. I was going places. Big places. And he was a skinny, dirty drunk.

Fast-forward 10 months. It was Christmastime. My long-distance relationship was at an impasse. I wanted to get married. He didn't. Now I was in a very, very bad place. A place where you feel not good enough. Not loved.

For some reason, I thought of that tortured soul from nearly a year ago, and I called his house. His girlfriend answered. I decided to act my age (22) and leave a message. It took her three weeks, but she told him I called. Not smart on her part. But fate works in mysterious ways.

He asked if I would spend the day with him. He'd built a house on family land, and wanted me to see it. I pictured a single-wide with uneven stairs and a roof made of mismatched shingles. I also remembered what he looked like the last time we met. My expectations were not high.

But the house was beautiful, and so was he. He'd gained weight. Cut his hair. Shaved.   Dressed in something other than dirty jeans, and I was smitten. We went to dinner, he got drunk and said in that sloppy, liquor-laden breathy way "I'm a gonna marry you. You just wait and see. I'm a gonna marry you "

"Okay, chief. Now tell me how to drive your truck. You can't drive, and I need to drive back to Greensboro in the morning."

I thought that was the end of it, but he was relentless. He gave me what I didn't have. Someone who wanted me. I didn't have a choice. He wouldn't take no for an answer.

I graduated in May, we were engaged in September, and married the next June. And that was it. The beginning of a very complicated relationship. Two opposites. We are both difficult personalities in our own way.

We both have our demons. His more obvious, mine within my head. Both of our demons have tried relentlessly to pull us apart, yet somehow we stick with it.

A Ride to Remember

My husband is not the most romantic man in the world. Don't get me wrong...he buys me more diamonds than I can wear in a week. Before we got married, he'd bring home roses for no reason. He picks out wonderful cards. But I'm pretty sure rednecks aren't allowed to be but so romantic.

With that said, I remember one of our first dates and can't help but laugh. He was taking me to dinner. Of course he was driving his obscenely large F350 teal dually. I'm thinking he must have eaten some sort of Mexican fare for lunch, or some other gassy cuisine, because he just couldn't hold it in.

Now that we're married, he thinks nothing of burning my nose hairs with his ass. But at the time, he tried to keep things smelling pleasant.

So we're driving down the road, and he says to me "I've got to pull over for a minute. I think I just crapped my pants." I reply "are you kidding me?"

Obviously not. He pulled the truck over, stuck his butt in the air, and asked me if his jeans had a spot.

Of course he didn't crap his pants. He's an adult, and adults don't crap their paints, right? Wrong.

Fast-forward about two years. We're newly married, and lying on the couch. I had my head in his lap, and smelled something funky. Being newly married, I didn't say anything, and in the back of my head worried if it was me.

The next night, I took my spot on the couch, my head again in his lap. And there it was. That smell. What the heck is that smell? Again, I went to bed and tried to not think about what it could be.

The next day I was sorting laundry, and came across the

offender. His comfy flannel pants that he wore at night. Apparently, someone had crapped their pants several nights ago, and never realized it.

How can an adult NOT realize crapping their pants? To this day I seriously have no idea. What I do know is that I gingerly picked them up by the pant cuff and ran to the outside trash can. That night I started laughing uncontrollably when I explained the smell, my reaction, and my discovery.

And my redneck husband proceeded to ask me why I threw the pants away. "They were really comfortable," he said. Yea. Too comfortable, if you ask me.

Wax and Whiskey

I love every hair on my redneck's head. I do not, however, love every hair on his back and ass. It's the opposite of romantic. And Jasen needs all the help he can muster in the romance department.

He could grow a mustache at 14 years old. He's down right burly in the winter when he "needs the hair for warmth," or in the summer when he just forgets to shave.

Shaving days just plain suck. He swears every time that he's cleaned up after himself. I beg to differ. I have to completely re-clean the entire bathroom sink. But really, that's okay. It's every other day of the week that gets to me.

He sheds. Constantly. In the shower, on the bathroom floor, in the closet. Two-inch black hairs. Undeniably his. And mine to clean up. If the floor is wet, I take a piece of toilet paper before I get into the shower, wipe down the floor, and toss it in the toilet. The vacuum doesn't like his hairs. Every now and then the drain clogs, and I sit there with a wire, cussing for an hour that he has enough hair on his back to make wigs.

Recently he decided to buy a mirror for the shower so he could shave with less mess. I envisioned a small, maybe 6-inch mirror. What do I find when I step into my shower? A 12in by 16in mirror. Basically, a full face and body mirror where I get to see every sagging inch of my body until the steam takes over and eases the image.

Once I decided to wax his back. I gave him a glass of whiskey on ice, and smeared hot, gooey, thick wax over his entire back. There was no turning back. I know it's sadistic, but that was my point. There would be no turning back. No strip of wonderfully smooth skin surrounded by the normal forest. I figured if we waxed his back, it would gradually get thinner. When I shave it, there's still stubble. Who knew men were wussies when it comes to beautification.

The first pull wasn't so bad. A shock, maybe, but not too bad. After that the whole experience (for him) went to hell.

"Holy mother of God that hurt! What the hell, babe!"

"Dude. Sip your drink. It's not that bad. Look...King of the Hill is on. Watch that and lay still."

"Just give me thirty seconds..."

He starts breathing like a woman in labor, grabs the rug, and holds on for dear life.

"Okay. Go!"

Riiiiiippp.

"Fuck. Am I bleeding?"

"Of course you're not bleeding. Grow up. Let's just get this over with."

Okay. I lied. He was definitely bleeding. Tiny drops of blood started pooling out of each pore. At this point, I began to laugh.

Uncontrollably. I don't know why. Maybe it's because women shave, we birth babies, we have yearly exams, and my Redneck Husband can't have his back waxed. Maybe it was his reaction...like I was scalping him. Maybe it was because he held his breath with each rip, and then cussed. I don't know. I just got tickled, and he did not find the situation as hilariously funny as I.

"Jesus Christ, honey. It's fucking hot in here. Can you turn up the A.C.?"

"Oh for the love of God."

I turn up the air conditioner, and return to my wax-o-pain.

Riiiiiipppppp.

"Okay! That's enough...you just pulled off a mole. And don't tell me I'm not bleeding. Get this shit off of me. Now. I'm done."

"Ummm...honey, there's no way to get it off. That's the point. We have to keep going. Otherwise you're just going to live with wax on your back. Suck it up, and lay down."

"Fuck. Just do them all. Turn up the television or something, so I can't hear myself scream. I can't believe I let you do this to me. You suck. I hate you right now."

"It's called Manscaping, honey. And I like a smooth back. It's sexy.

You like smooth legs, I like smooth backs. Okay...hold on."

Riiiipppp.

"I don't care if I'm not sexy. I'm a man, damn it. I'm supposed to be hairy."

"Not this hairy, honey. This is ridiculous."

"Fuck you and your wax. This sucks. I'm never doing this again. You tricked me."

Yep...sure did...and it's friggin hilarious.

Chapter 2: Romance...or Lack Thereof

My husband's favorite words. "Come on, giiiiirrrrl...let me see that ass." Unfortunately, this is not romance to me. Or to Pigtunia the hog, whom he speaks to the same way. Apparently I and Pigtunia are on the same level as far as the women in his life. Me and Pigtunia...showing that ass.

You Must have been a Real Heifer

I lost about 20 pounds after our wedding. Jasen looked at me and said "So how much weight have you lost?" I answered, "20 pounds."

"Wow babe. You must've been a real heifer before. I never noticed..."

Okay. How the hell am I supposed to take that? Chalk it up to Redneck idiotness?

My problem with weight is that no matter how much or how little the scale reads, I'll never feel happy inside my skin. Never have, never will. I've realized this, and decided to try and move on. But seriously. Calling me a cow? Not helping!

A Love Note for the Redneck Husband

I took Juni to Great Wolf Lodge on a Thursday. Jasen stayed with us that night, but headed back Friday. So it was the "Juni & Mommy Road Trip of 2012." And it was awesome. Since then it's become a tradition – Juni & Mommy Road Trips to Great Wolf each year This particular time I probably gained 5 pounds noshing on pancakes, waffles and ice cream for breakfast, lunch and dinner. We bowled, played in the arcade, and swam until our fingers and toes were nice and prune-y.

I figured Jasen would burp beer and fart turnips all night without me there to kick him in the kidneys, but I still wanted him to know I was thinking about him. I know how he gets into bed...like a walrus plops onto a rock. No attention to the pretty pillows or sweet-smelling sheets. Just a humph and a plop. And snoring. Lots and lots of snoring.

A note atop his pillow wouldn't work. So where do you place a note for your Redneck Husband? I decided to think of where he spends his time.

The toilet? Putting a note on the toilet seat just seemed wrong. Very, very wrong. The fridge? I'm thinking he's seeing only food when the door opens. My note would get trampled. On the vanity, by his deodorant? I was out of town...no telling if he'd touch the Arm & Hammer that day or not. By the beer would definitely work, but he may decide to break out the Jack Daniels with me out of town. His truck is a mess, and it smells funny. Plus his idea of taking a message consists of tiny pieces of paper strewn throughout the entire vehicle. His sock and underwear drawer? Again...I'm out of town. He could wear his long johns all weekend for all I knew.

I decided my best bet was inside the shower, on top of his Pantene. I know. Not extremely romantic, but it's the only thing I knew he'd do while I was out of town...I knew that after a day in the waterpark, he'd take a shower. It worked.

That night I called him because Juni was crying, missing Daddy. And Jasen said he found the note, and that it made him feel good. Point scored for the wife. Point scored for Redneck Husband once he settled Juni down.

Chapter 3: Juni

They say you change when you have a child. Yes, my tits are heavy and need an industrial-strength bra to lift them to their rightful place. Yes, I have a bit of a baby belly, which has now lasted 12 years. And yes, I have cellulite. My legs jiggle. My ass jiggles. My arms jiggle. But the most extraordinary change is not in my body, but in my soul.

I'm talking learning the meaning of life type of change. The love you feel for your child is inexplicable to someone who isn't a parent. It was to me, anyway, until Jasen Edward Norge, Jr. (or Juni, for family and close friends) came into this world. He weighed just 6.9 pounds but ripped me from end to end. Too much information? Just wait. I'm full of information. I already keep panty liners in my purse for the impromptu trips to the trampoline park…apparently, my future holds Depends. But whatever. It is what it is. As was the pregnancy and delivery.

I'm Pregnant

And I'm terrified. You see, I'm a bit of a psychiatric Guinea pig. I now take six psychiatric medications…but I digress. My mental health weaves its way in and out of my everyday life and I've learned to live with it. Diagnosis? Bipolar I with mild disassociation, general anxiety disorder, and acute panic disorder.

The Redneck Husband and I had been married for three years when we decided it was time to have a child. I was 28, he was 29. But my panic made even decided to stop taking birth control a huge obstacle.

I'd stop taking the pills, and within days have a series of attacks, get scared, and take all of the missed doses at once.

After four months of fighting with myself I stopped taking

the pills. Three months later I found myself curled up on the bathroom floor with the positive pregnancy test, having the worst panic attack of my life.

I'd assumed pregnancy would trigger some level of anxiety, but I could never have prepared myself for the extent of my panic.

The night I took the test, I was too scared to take my Xanax for the attack. I had to wait it out. All night.

First thing the next morning my husband made a call to my doctor. Apparently he was out of town, but my husband was so persistent he spoke with him via cell phone while he was in an airplane.

I don't remember much from the first three weeks of my pregnancy, other than that I was miserable. I was taking up to 4mg of Xanax daily and Tylenol PM at night. But all of the medication barely took the edge off. I was worried about the effects of the medication on the baby, but my doctor said he was more worried that I would miscarry from the stress of the attacks.

I'd sit on the couch with my cat Max in my lap, rocking back and forth. I'd play a handheld Tetris game all day and watch t.v. I didn't brush my hair. I didn't put on makeup. I didn't get dressed. I lost 14 pounds in two weeks.

When things got really bad, I'd start telling my husband that "I just wanted things back the way they were." I vividly remember him telling me I didn't have to stay pregnant. We could adopt. Or we could stay just the two of us. He was at his wits end, crying, and hopelessly trying to help me.

I would have moments of clarity, where I realized I did want the baby, and that this was just a panic attack, but they were far and few between. I was scared of being pregnant, what it would do to my body and my marriage. I was scared to have this tiny person to take care of and raise. I was scared of everything.

I later found out that my doctor wanted to have me admitted to a psychiatric hospital, but that my husband refused to sign the papers.

I don't remember exactly when I began to feel better. It was gradual. One day I realized I hadn't taken as much medication that day as the one before, and by the time I was seven months along I wasn't taking anything for acute attacks.

The Delivery

Imagine being in labor. My water broke 12 hours earlier, and

I'm now in the throes of the devil – Pitocin. The contractions are two minutes apart and lasting two minutes each. My math isn't great, but my contractions were giving me no break. I held onto the cold metal rod on the side of the bed, closed my eyes, and moaned. I was dilated 2 cm. I was crying. It felt like I was under water – not able to make out voices or faces, but hearing mumbles and seeing blurs of family members. Family members my sister abruptly kicked out when the shit hit the fan. The shit hits the fan a lot around here, which you'll soon find out. But this was the first real test.

Jasen paced in the shadows in front of me, crying. "Dude. Knock it off. You're not fucking helping!!" "I can't. You're in so much pain and I can't help you," he mumbled through his tears. At this point I'm thinking I just want him to shut his pie hole so I can get an epidural and get this childbirth deal over with. So I offer him two Xanax pills. He takes them. What I didn't tell him was that I had two prescriptions – one for .5 mg, one for 2 mg. My sister, following my request, handed my husband 4 mg of Xanax. He slept until it was time for me to push eight hours later.

Everyone was asleep, it's about 2:30 am, and I have to take a poop. I also can't put my left leg down – it's propped in the air. I wake my sister, and tell her I have to take the biggest poop in the world. CeCe, the common sensed sister, asked if she could take a peek. "Seriously, I just have to poop." "Ummm…no. He's crowning. I see…I don't know what I see, but we need a fucking nurse." The nurse comes in and immediately calls the doctor. Jasen springs to life, and before I know what's happening, I'm rolled on my left side when not pushing. I see the heart rate going up and down, but I don't think anything of it. I push and feel the burn. Skipping through the pooping on the table, ripping from end to end and the lovely goo that comes out of the female body during and after giving birth, 20 minutes later, our little man was here. The cord had a true knot, so Jasen couldn't cut it – they cut it while the baby was still inside. He was tiny. Breakable, almost. And perfect.

Baby Juni

The redneck husband called our son Juni for the first time when he was about three weeks old, and the name just stuck. I'm sure he's thrilled the world knows his nickname, but such is the life of an author's son.

Crying. And more crying. And more crying.

That kid did not stop screaming for 10 months. His epiglottis flap wasn't formed since he was three weeks early, and he had severe reflux. But instead of spitting up, Juni decided to swallow the nastiness and scream his bloody head off until everyone in the house was at their wit's end. He slept in the swing, or with me in the rocker. If he laid down, the reflux would hit and he'd wake up, and the process began again. For 10 months he woke up every 45 minutes screaming for food. I nursed for 16 months. It was amazing, and I loved every second of it. Except for the time he had reflux while nursing and snatched his head back without unlatching, leaving my nipple stretching with his retching body. Or the time he bit me while pulling my hair. Or my personal favorite, the time when he sucked off a skin tag on my areola. I guess he saved me a trip to the dermatologist.

I tried everything to get that kid to sleep. One night I crawled into the handmade crib, every nail driven by my husband, and slept in a ball next to my baby. If I wasn't there, he wasn't asleep. It wreaked havoc on our lives. I was exhausted, Jasen was exhausted. We were at our whit's end.

One night, Juni just would not stop crying. Jasen asked what he could do and I snapped "Nothing! There's nothing YOU can do to help. Do you have nipples? Then fuck off." Then one night, when Juni was about 4 weeks old, he and the Redneck Husband bonded. I needed a bath and a few hours of sleep. I handed our bundle of screaming joy to the Redneck, and told him "whatever you do, don't mess with me. I need a bath. A real bath. With bubbles. And I need some sleep. Real sleep. Like two hours." So I went upstairs, drew my lovely bath, slipped into the steamy water, closed my eyes, and heard the sweet sound of silence. For about 12 seconds. Then the screaming began. It's around this time when I'm thinking I should have locked the door. Jasen runs upstairs and into the bathroom, which is now filled with chilly February air. "He won't stop crying!" "No shit honey. That's why I need some time. Give him a bottle – I pumped earlier." Ten minutes later I hear the crying again, and in comes the Redneck. "What the fuck is wrong with him? He won't stop crying. I burped him, I changed him, and he doesn't want another bottle. He just wants to scream." "Yeah, honey. Welcome to my world. That's just what he does. He screams. I deal with it all day long. Now get out and let me have a freaking bath!" I'm in the bath, but I can hear the screaming. It's very relaxing. Five minutes later, it's quiet. Eerily quiet. Jasen walks in, bare-chested and cradling his infant son softly in his arms, skin to skin. Little Juni had stopped crying. And my husband had started. He came into the bathroom, tears down his cheeks. "I don't know why, but I took off my shirt and his onesie, and put him on my chest. He just stopped crying." I looked at my proud husband and loved him more than the moment before. He had instincts. And they worked. I slept for two full hours that night. And it was awesome. Five years later, Juni slept through the night for the first time.

Juni said his first word around his first birthday. DaDa. Of course. Then it was dactor. Then MaMo. Once he started talking, he didn't stop. And let me tell you, this kid is hilarious.

Jackass

When we had Juni, I definitely felt worried about Jasen's language. He's a four-letter word lover. So I'm seeing myself constantly picking at him, telling him not to teach Juni to say this or that. So of course it would be me that taught him my favorite word...

Jackass

I call Jasen a jackass at least three times a week. This is down from five times a day before Juni and I visited my dad, and this happened:

Juni wanted to go outside. My dad didn't. He told him to wait patiently. Juni looked at my dad, gave him a pout face, turned around on his heels and said (with my kind of attitude) "jackass." My dad, his wife and I couldn't help but laugh. Still...did jackass have to be the first rude word he learned? Couldn't it have been one of Jasen's favorites? argh.

Juni-isms

I love the honesty in children. From day one, they make no excuses. If they're hurt, they cry. If they're tired, they sleep. If they're hungry, they eat. That honesty amazes me daily.

Juni is beautifully, brutally honest. Like the time when he said "Mommy...I love your big fat belly. It's just so warm and soft. Mmmmm."

Thanks, son.

Here are a few others:

Maybe I puke tonight: He says this at least 12 times a day. He gets it from Jasen, who says this line after just about every dinner.

You be kidding me: He gets this one from me. I say "Are you kidding me?" at least 12 times a day either to him or Jasen. Jasen farts at least once during dinner every night and blames it on Juni... Are you kidding me? Juni paints the walls with blue Avon sunscreen... Are you kidding me? The calves get out and are staring at me... Are you kidding me? The paint I applied two days ago starts randomly coming off in huge latex-like sheets...are you freaking kidding me???

I want it already: pretty much this means he wants something now, and we're about to have a massive tantrum.

It looks like a dragon tail: his description of a gigantic poop.

I go wish you: I go with you

Is dat an idea?: This would be Juni's bargaining tool - is that a good idea? If someone tells him no, he turns on his debate skills.

Little minutes, mama. Just little minutes: I want to stay here longer

One day, my grandmother Corky asked Juni if he had to potty, since his hands were grabbing his crotch. "No. I just scratchin' my balls."

Excellent. Thank God my Corky didn't hear or understand him. She's the most uber-conservative, ultra-mannered woman I know.

Juni is slowly learning social etiquette's, which makes my job less embarrassing. But at the same time, it makes me a little sad. He's learning to not be completely honest at every moment. He's learning not to speak his mind every chance he gets. He'll learn the cool dance moves instead of moving his toddler body so freely to the music. In short, he'll grow up. Which is wonderful and sad mixed together. But at least he won't be telling his great-grandmother about scratching his balls.

Much Ado about Balls

One of Juni's favorite things is the human anatomy. Boobies and balls, in particular. We're working on learning that: 1. boobies are for babies, and 2. Juni is not a baby.

I leave the balls discussion to Jasen, and this is what I'm left with:

1. We're eating sushi with Jasen and my sister. Juni comes back from the bathroom with my sister and announced that he has balls and his aunt does not have balls. Then he continues to point to

each patron in the restaurant, stating whether or not each person has balls.

2. Juni, Jasen and an older friend of Jasen's are riding in a truck. All are in the front seat when Juni points out that: I have balls. My daddy has balls. My daddy has big balls. I have little balls.

Argh....

Body Comparisons, Juni Style

I laughed until I almost wet my pants. Here's why: Juni's best friend came over one day while his mom was at work, since school was closed. The boys absolutely love each other. They played at the swings and in the sand pile. They created a bird's nest out of leaves, sticks, acorns and mud, and then used even more mud to glue it to the back porch handrail (thank you for that, PBS) They took the dog for a "walk" and visited what they call Mud World. Mud World is really just the ditch behind out house. But believe me, the name fits. The two mud daubers trotted up to the back door and stood in my kitchen, dripping with deep, dark, gray goo. They were stripping off their clothes with grimy hands, and laughing hysterically. Completely naked, covered in mud, and laughing.

I grew up behind a borrow pit, which is basically one giant mud hole. I couldn't get mad at them, but I also couldn't hose them down, either. All I could do was laugh.

I put clean socks on one, and carried the other straight upstairs to the bathroom. The second the water began filling the tub, it turned brown from the mud.

While the tub filled, Juni's best friend's mom showed up to take him home, and we searched for Sadie, who apparently still had her leash attached and was busy walking herself. It's unlike her to not come when called. But I found her, drenched in mud, pouting in the front yard, still attached to her once hot-pink but now completely muddied leash. Poor little pooch. As a side note, I have no idea how she managed it, but she came inside later that night, completely clean, dry, and smelling nothing like mud. Amazing.

When us mommies returned upstairs we found the boys, 85% clean, and toweling themselves off. And this is when the fun really begins...

Juni "Mommy...he has a little bellybutton, and I have a big bellybutton."

Friend "Yeah! I like my belly button."

Me "Yes, Juni. Everyone is made different. And both of your

belly buttons are adorable."

Juni (pointing to his friend and examining himself) "Mommy...he has a short, skinny pee pee. Mine is long and fat."

Friend "Yeah! And mine is fat right here (lower belly)."

Other mother and I: Absolutely, positively speechless. Not because we couldn't think of anything to say, but because we were both laughing so hard it was physically impossible to speak a single syllable.

Car Conversations

Juni and I spend a lot of time in the car. That's what happens when you live on the outskirts of civilization. We rock out, we roll the windows down, and we talk. Some our best conversations take place in the car. Questions abound. "Mommy, what my finger made of?" "Mommy, when I gonna get bigger?" "Mommy, you do dat when you a girl?"

"Mommy, you know daddy when he a boy?"

Some questions are better than others...

Mommy.

Yes, Juni?

Everybody die?

Yes, Juni. Everybody dies.

(short pause) Mommy.

Yes, Juni?

Everybody die when they get old?

Yes, Juni. Everybody dies when they get very, very old.

(longer pause) Mommy...Nanny and PaPa very, very old you know. They gonna die aday (today)?

No, Juni. Not today.

(pretty long pause this time) Mommy...when you gonna die?

No time soon, baby. Mommy's not old yet.

Mommy...you old, you know.

Thanks for that, son. Seriously. I'm not old.

(a minute later) Mommy...Shelby die, you know.

Yes, Juni. I know.

I miss her, you know. I love my new puppy Sadie, but I still miss my old dog, Shelby. I miss playing with her, you know.

I know, Juni. I miss her, too. (now I have a lump in my throat – Shelby was my dog from college)

You ran ober (over) her with the car, you know.

Okay! Enough talk about death. Seriously, son. At this point, I'll talk about anything else. Politics? Religion? Where do babies come from? Take your pick.

Mommy...I already know where babies come from, you know.

Um...Okay.

Mommies get big bellies and den (then) poop dem (them) out. Just like the chickens poop out eggs and cows poop out baby cows.

Um...okay. who told you that, baby?

Daddy did. Mommy...when you gonna poop out your baby?

Excuse me? I'm not pregnant, Juni. I'm not pooping out any babies any time soon. Can we maybe talk about death again?

Alright, Mommy. But you do have a big belly, you know.

Thanks, Juni ... Okay! Unbuckle your belt...we're here! Thank the lord...

The Mole

Juni was scratching Jasen's back one night, and apparently

scratched off a mole. One of those red, weird looking things. Benign. Pretty much every time I shave Jasen's back I usually nip a few, unintentionally. Which is why he basically doesn't let me near his back side with a razor.

So Juni scratches off the mole. I tell Jasen to get it checked out, because that's what my dermatologist had always told me; that if you injure a mole, it can easily become infected and can change the makeup of the cells. Raises the chance of cancer or something.

Of course Jasen says he's fine. The next day, he comes home.

"Babe, can you come in here?"

"What is it? That bump on your head is NOT a tick. I've looked at it a million times. And I'm not looking at anything on your butt. Get a mirror."

"I want you to look at this thing on my back. It hurts like hell. But you have to promise not to touch it."

There is only one way to describe what was left of the mole. A giant, very full cow tick. They're gray, bulbous, and just plain nasty.

"Ummm....honey, this doesn't look so good. It looks like an inflated cow tick. I think you should see a doctor. And it's all red around it."

"It's fine. As long as nothing touches it, it's fine."

The next day we take Juni to a birthday pool party. Jasen wears a white shirt, and sits in a high-backed chair. He gets up looking like a mobster has stabbed him square in the back.

"Babe, will you look at my mole? It itches."

"Holy Hell, Jasen. It looks like someone's stabbed you. Get in the house before you scare the kids."

The blood had mixed with the sweat, run down his back, and soaked the waistband in his shorts.

"Just put a band aid on it. It's fine."

"It's not fine! You look like you should be on the Sopranos! Go. To. The. DOCTOR. Now. Otherwise, the sympathy is gone."

Two days later, Jasen comes home during lunch and swipes on extra deodorant. He's having his moles checked. An hour later, I get a few texts. Remember, My Redneck Husband has huge sausage fingers, so texting is not his thing.

"Carp [crap]. They want me no clothes. I got no underwear on. What I do?"

"Ha! What the hell is wrong with you? Didn't your mom

teach you to always wear your undies to the doctor? Ask for a paper blanket or something. A paper towel. A napkin. Anything."

"Shut [shit]. Here comes doc."

Thirty minutes later he calls.

"Babe. It was horrible. I can hear the nurses laughing, and in comes the most beautiful woman in the world. Seriously. Of course, I had to have this 25-year-old doctor, and there I am naked-assed. It was horrible."

I start laughing. And them remember...shouldn't I be the most beautiful woman in the world? I give him shit for the slip-up, but really it's just too funny. It would be like Brad Pit (before he was all shaggy) coming in for my yearly girlie appointment.

"It was horrible, babe. I started to sweat and everything. I felt like an idiot."

"You didn't wear underwear. You are an idiot. How's the mole?"

"Gone. She took it off...said it looked like it was getting infected. But she checked everything else out, and all the other moles are good to go."

"Lovely, honey. Hey...can I shave your back tonight?"

"Fuck no. What's for dinner?"

Bird, Mouse and Cat: Three Doomed Fish

To describe those years when Juni didn't sleep as exhausting would be a gross understatement. There are no words to describe. At one point I thought he had some terrible stomach disorder. Nope. Reflux. I tried a vibrating crib. One of those bears that emits a heartbeat and sloshing sounds like the womb. A wedge to elevate his head. Then pillows under his crib mattress to elevate his entire top half. Nothing worked.

He slept in his swings for the first six months of his life. And when I say slept, I basically mean cat naps in between screaming fits. At the urging of his pediatrician, we Ferberized him at 10 months. Pitiful, but he did learn to fall asleep on his own, and would stay that way. For approximately 2 hours. And then I had to repeat the process.

I'd fall asleep sitting beside his crib, on the floor, so that when he did scream it wouldn't wake up my husband. I'd fall asleep nursing him in the rocker. I'd fall asleep while he played on the floor. I'd fall asleep just about anywhere.

Even at four years old, Juni rarely slept through the night. He woke up screaming for me, saying he's scared. One week it was deers. The next it was the blinds on his window. Or the little closet door. Or just nothing. He'd wake up because his overnight pull-up leaked. Which isn't just a quick kiss and back to bed. It's changing clothes, sheets, pillows. All at 4 a.m.

Sleeping in the Norge house is miserable. Even though Jasen doesn't get up with Juni, it still wakes him, and I have to hear about it in the morning.

Eventually I hit my breaking point. I was falling asleep in his bed again, in the middle of the night. Which just plain sucks. The kid sleeps like a crazy person. I'd wake up, sweating from his plastic mattress cover, his feet lodged in my spine, me tinkering on the edge of the mattress clutching Beary. Sucked. Big time.

And so I resorted to bribery. I am now a full-fledged, card-carrying supporter of bribery. It's amazing, really. One day after a visit to the local aquarium, Juni asks for a fish tank. That night, I bribe him: "you sleep in your bed all night, without screaming your head off, and you can get a fish tank." He's definitely allowed to come into my bedroom if he's scared or doesn't feel well, but screaming like someone's stabbing him with a butter knife is out of the question. As a child who suffered from night terrors her entire childhood, this troubled me a bit, but I also realize how rare night terrors are, and work hard every day to not project my anxiety onto him.

My point is, the bribery worked. The first night he woke up once. Ran into my room, sounding like an elephant, but no screams. I led him back to his bed, and within 2 minutes he was snoring just like Daddy. Friday made three weeks with no screaming. Jackpot! So we headed to the locally-owned pet store.

Three fish later, and we were ready to roll. He named them Mouse, Cat and Bird. Adorable. He fed them, decorated their little tank. and stood on the same wooden stool I stood on as a child, staring at them and talking to them.

It was wonderful. My plan had worked. Bwahahaha!

And then, disaster. The yellow fish went belly up.

"Mommy...what wrong with that fish? He sleeping?"

I figured Juni could handle it. He's seen dead chickens, cows, snakes, unfortunately, he even saw me run over my dog, Shelby, and reminds me of my murderous act at least once a week.

So the kid understands that animals die. So I told him the truth. "Okay. I get a new one? Not a yellow one, though. They no good. I want a guppy. A whole family, so they can have babies. Alright?" Alright, Juni. I'll go back tomorrow and get you a whole guppy family.

And then as I snuck his sleeping body into his bed, I saw it. Three floaters. Damn it! I had single-handily murdered Bird, Cat and Mouse. They were stuck in the plastic plants. They looked like they were sleeping, so I went with it. Told Juni they were so tired from the trip.

I was so upset when I got into bed, Jasen actually sat straight up at one point and said "Fuck the fucking fish! They're fucking fish for Christ's sake! Jesus! Just go to bed. You didn't mean to do it. He'll get over it." And then as he laid down, rolled over and closed his eyes I heard him grumble "Damn fucking fish."

Okay. I get it. It was like a cheesy sitcom where the hamster dies and the parents run out, looking for the twin to said hamster. Something I never thought I would ever do.
And yet, first chance I got, I snuck out of the house, found said twin fishes, and bought them. I spent $15 on water conditioners, including

one with live bacteria to make their home the perfect fishy habitat. Then I bought two gallons of spring water, just to spoil the little buggars.

And so now, what began as a $30 bribery is now up to $50. But this morning, Juni woke up, asking to see his fish first thing, and I didn't have to lie and say there were napping. They were alive, happy, and waiting to be fed. It's amazing what we'll do for our children. We don't want to see them hurt, even if it is over a fucking fish. We want to see them happy, rewarded, and succeed. And with the newly named Cat, Mouse, Bird, C and J fluttering their happy little fins, I can officially stand at the top of my stairs and shout "Victorious!" I have made fish live! For more than 12 hours! Woo. Friggin. Hoo, baby!

The Great Pooptastrophe of 2009 (and other innard exerpts)

It's amazing how our lives change with children. Whatever seems important in their world at the moment suddenly becomes paramount in our lives. Our everyday lives revolve around these tiny creatures and their entry into the world.

I assumed potty training would go like every other milestone in Juni's life: he'd find a way to make it as difficult as possible, but throw in a few laughs for comic relief and to keep me sane. I was correct.

Juni takes after his dad. No bladder control. And he has taken to peeing outdoors. And I'm not talking about on a tree in the woods. I'm talking about off our front porch. In front of my uber-clean friend, and at the beach on a holiday weekend.

He shows no shame. He once pulled his swim trunks down in front of my germaphobe friend and pooped in the rocks beside the pool. I asked him what he thought he was doing, and he replied "it's okay mommy. Just squirt the water gun up my butt, and Duchess (our dog) will eat my poop." I didn't even know what to say after that.

Then there was the time he proclaimed "mommy! daddy! Come watch me poop! It's gonna be a big one!" When a potty training toddler asks you to check out his business, you check out his business. And I've got to admit...it was huge. Of epic proportions.

And there was the time he had an accident in his undies, and while in transit from the undies to the toilet the poop took an unexpected detour...to my son's head. It smacked him right upside the forehead. To this day I don't know how that happened, but it did. It bounced off his head and plopped itself right in the toilet. A perfect landing.

After a particularly large sushi meal of avocado roll, my husband once beckoned me into the bathroom to show off his son's prized poop. "Mommy! It's as big as a dragon's tail," Juni proclaimed. My redneck husband was so proud.

But nothing compares to the Pooptastrophe. Nothing.

I'll be the first to admit that the Pooptastrophe was my fault. Mine and Levi Strauss. Whomever decided it was a good idea to fasten a size 4t pair of jeans with a button in lieu of a snap needs to be slapped. Hard. With a large, dead fish. Right in their big, fat, non-toddler-thinking mouth.

Juni was just learning to center himself on the toilet. "I need privacy" became his favorite bathroom saying. And he meant it. The kid likes his privacy. So he'd sneak into the bathroom, and call me when he was ready for a good butt wipe. Never leave the job of wiping up to the toddler. You will absolutely find three results: a great loss of toilet paper followed by a severely clogged toilet, and a toddler with his finger in his ass, telling everyone who will listen that his butt itches. But I digress.

It was early morning, and I was busy checking the business email upstairs. I heard him close the bathroom door, which meant it was poop time. Then I heard him say "mommy! I need you help me peeze..." Of course I assumed he needed a wipe. I obviously assumed wrong. Very wrong.

You see, when a four-year-old boy has to poop, he waits until the last possible moment before leaving his toys. Using the toilet serves no purpose to that four-year-old, other than to interrupt his playing tractors. And so therefore, there is a very limited amount of time between when he begins moving toward the bathroom, and when the turtle head starts to pop out.

I hopped down the stairs about 30 seconds later and was hit in the face with two things. First, the smell of a very ripe bathroom. Second, the sight of my son, his urine-soaked pants around his ankles, a giant turd resting in his underwear, and his hands reaching down to pick it up.

Before I could mutter even the beginning of the word "stop!" Juni had grabbed the log, tossed it in the toilet, and was unravelling the toilet paper.

He'd made it to the potty on time only to find that his new pants didn't have a snap, but a grown-up button. He fumbled with the button, and my bathroom paid the price. I stripped him of his clothes, disinfected his hands, and began to scrub down the bathroom.

Too bad I didn't give him specific instructions to NOT make his own breakfast while I was cleaning up after the Great Pooptastrophe. When I finished the bathroom, I had a box of Nesquick, a bag of cereal, and a gallon of milk to mop off the floor.

Most of my experiences with Juni the Toddler make me laugh. Some make me cry. Others, like the Great Pooptastrophe of 2009, leave me in stitches. I learned something extremely important through the Pooptastrophe: Never ask a potty training toddler, especially a boy, to "hold on just a sec."

Running down the Driveway, Chicken in Hand and Toddler in Tow

This one time, not at band camp, I thought it would be a good idea to take my favorite chicken, Gladys, on a little field trip. Juni could learn about what chickens eat, and I could enjoy the weather.

We decided the best place for this trip would be the back yard, where I could pick up the bricks that border the flower beds and Juni could find bugs. Juni and I walked down the driveway to the chicken pen, a carried her back up to the house.

Problem was that it was windy outside, and the inflatable bouncer was still out from the Easter egg hunt. The bouncer was high-tailing it down the driveway from the wind, headed toward the road. So I started to run, chicken in hand, and Juni in tow. Gladys was flapping her wings, screeching in my ear, while I hauled the bouncer back up to the house and stuffed it into the garage.

That was my exercise for the day.

Stretch Marks

I've had stretch marks since puberty. They're light and faded, or so I though.

I'm weeding in a pair of shorts, bending over and feel something tickling the back of my booty. I, realizing it's not a curious bug, I jolt and yelp: "Juni! What the heck, man? That tickles! And it's actually a little inappropriate."

Juni says: "I not mean to tickle you, Momma. I just lookin'.

Momma. What dem lines on your legs?"

Me: "Huh?"

Juni: "You know, dem scratches on your legs."

Me: "Juni. What in the world are you talking about?"

Juni, touching my legs again: "These, Momma! Cat scratch you?"

Me: "No, Juni. Those are stretch marks. Thanks for noticing."

Juni: "What stretched your legs, Momma?"

Me: "You did, son. You did."

Juni: "Oh. Okay, Momma. Sorry I did dat."

I hate my legs, but I absolutely love my kid.

Vodka Water

I bought my kiln for pottery before I found a wheel. To offset my pottery withdrawal, I played with glass for a bit; especially bottle slumping. Jasen poured vodka into a water bottle, tossed it in the freezer, and forgot about it. Apparently he did this so I could have the bottle.

Last week he packed a cooler for a day trip, and tossed in the water bottle, oblivious to the fact that it was, in fact, raspberry vodka. Cheap raspberry vodka.

"Mommy...taste this water, please. There's something wrong with it."

"It's water, Juni. I'm sure it's fine."

"Seriously, Mommy. Taste this. Please."

"Ugh! Okay. Hand me the bottle."

I take a swig, and immediately spew sticky raspberry vodka across the dashboard.

"What the Hell, Jasen? This is friggin vodka! Juni, are you okay buddy? Did you swallow it?"

"No, I spit it back in the bottle. My tongue burns dough."

"Awe, buddy, I'm sorry. Jasen ... I am NOT cleaning this dashboard. Your vodka, your mess."

"It's okay. Daddy ... alcohol is nasty. You shouldn't drink it. Mommy ... does vodka kill little boys?"

"No, Juni, it doesn't. It just burns your tongue."

"Whew. I fought I might get killed by it."

Fast forward a few weeks. Juni is my little golf-a-holic, in his second clinic of the summer. He gets into the car, it's almost 100 degrees out, and I hand him a bottled water.

Apparently, it resembled the vodka water bottle.

"Mommy, is this odka water?"

"Huh?"

"ODKA water...is this ODKA water?"

"What? Say it slower, Juni."

"VODKA. WATER. Is this VODKA WATER. You know, that nasty stuff Daddy drinks."

"No, Juni. It's not vodka water. You're cool, dude. I threw that out and made Daddy promise to keep his vodka water out of the freezer."

Chapter 4: Animal House of Steroids

Growing up I had dogs, cats and a horse. I did not like the horse, and the horse did like me. Until I married the Redneck Husband, I'd had no other contact with farm animals. What a surprise I was in for.

i. Am. WONDER WOMAN...

I woke one morning feeling like I'd been run over by a Mac

truck head-on. And smacked by a train from the other end. Then left to die between the two. My entire body screamed with aches. I slithered out of bed. I almost poked my eye out with the mascara wand, because my fingers can't grip anything. Total muscle exhaustion in every inch of every muscle from my ears to my pinkie toe. And it feels awesome. Almost as awesome as the night before.

I delivered Buttercup's calf the night before. I know. Not something I'd ever consider in my realm of possibility. But I did it. Me. ME! Me. The sister who wears makeup every day. Even to the gym. Me. The girl who has too many shoes. None of which are covered in anything stinky. Me. The one who doesn't pick the chicken eggs because the coup makes me gag. ME!

I'd spent the day making pickles, doing the laundry, mowing the lawn, and hanging out with Juni's friend Kyle and his mom Grace. I love Grace and Juni loves Kyle. A match made in preschool heaven. Grace loves animals as much as I do, so when I noticed Buttercup by herself, circling and contracting, we both hooked the boys up with a cartoon and snacks, and we plopped a squat in the field, armed with a zoom lensed camera and optimistic excitement.

Thirty minutes later the boys were running in the back yard,

Buttercup had passed the bubble (her water breaking) and two hooves were sticking out of her by just inches. Wonderful. Just friggin wonderful. We both decided to head to the house, watch from the window, and have my cell phone ready to dial the vet. Thirty minutes after that, and I knew it was time to make the call. Calves can't take much labor. After an hour things get sketchy. Two hours, and all bets are off.

I called the emergency large animal vet over at The Oaks...I love them. Strong, kick-ass women with awesome attitudes. This was the second call I'd made in as many weeks. And I didn't want the same result as the last. Unfortunately, the vet was an hour-and-a-half away from my home. Fabulous. There was a possibility she could save the calf. I really didn't want to go through delivering a dead animal again. It's just not my style. So I asked her what I could do.

"Anything you can do with your hands and body strength won't hurt either one of them," she explained. "It's when you start using chains and come-a-longs that you can get yourself into a mess."

Fabulous. But that wasn't the best part...Jasen wasn't home. I dialed his cell. At least an hour before he'd roll down the driveway.

My first thought? The f-bomb. Damn it! I am SO not cut out for this.

And then I looked out the window and saw Buttercup, mooing in pain, pushing for all she was worth, with no progress.

So I traded in my comfy pants for a pair of Levi's and slipped on my barn boots, which I wear maybe once a year. If it snows. Of course I forgot socks. Because who has time to run upstairs? Not me.

I decided I was going to do this full-out, or not at all. So I rolled under the hot wire. I rolled up my sleeves, and slowly walked up to Buttercup.

Here's something to know about this cow. She's friggin huge. A good 1500 pounds of pregnant, heaving, mooing bovine. But she's calm.

The bull, on the other hand, was not. He immediately trotted through the ditch with curiosity. I waved a stick at him. Yeah right. Big John is a ton of fun. Literally. He weighs a ton. I'm in the field, between a laboring cow and her 2,000 lb. baby daddy, and he's dancing around me, trying to get to the action. So I ripped part of a 3-inch tree out of the ground, chased after him, and threw it at his head once he crossed the ditch. And wouldn't you know it...I hit square on. He shook his curly-haired fat head, bucked and kicked and turned his fat ass around. Phew.

Buttercup was standing. So I inched up behind her, and knelt down. Luckily cows can only kick to the side. She bent her head around and sniffed me. It's important to note something about a cow's nose at this point. It's not cute and cuddly like a horse. It's wet. And drooly. And snotty. And I didn't care.

She heaved down to the ground with the next contraction, and I grabbed hold of the hooves. Holy slipperiness. She tried to get up, so I patted her hip, and spoke to her like I would an injured dog. And she understood. She began to push, and I began to pull. And nothing moved, except me. I pulled so hard on the slippery hooves that I flew to the ground, on my ass, in cow crap. Excellent. I needed a towel. But was wearing a shirt. Good enough.

I wiped the hooves while she relaxed. I dug my boots into the ground, and sat. The next contraction, I effing pulled. And a little came out. So I wiped with my shirt, and pulled again. Inch by inch, wipe by wipe, I got to the knees.

And then all progress stopped. Fabulous. Without thinking, I dove into the abyss. Up to my biceps in cow who-who. I grabbed on behind the knees, and heaved them out after the next set of contractions. But the head was stuck. She'd pushed so much with no progression that her cervix was swollen. I'd learned this from What to Expect when You're Expecting. It creates a ring, and the head can't come out.

Okay. So I knew what the problem was. And I knew how to fix it. The how to was what freaked me out. But what the hell. She'd pooped on me, I had amniotic liquid and goo on me, and I was sweating like a pig. No going back now.

So I stretched and rubbed and massaged while she relaxed, and pulled her open, allowing the tongue and nose to come through. The tongue sticks out because the contractions are so strong that it pushes all of the fluids out of the lungs, along with the tongue. I took a break, and noticed that the tongue was blue. And licking its lips. Holy cow...the calf was alive. I shouted to Grace, and the adrenaline kicked in full force.

I shoved both arms in to my biceps again, put my heels against her ass, and friggin pulled like I've never pulled before. She mooed and pushed. I growled and pulled. And talked to Buttercup like she could understand me. This calf was alive. I was not going to have the vet turn up with it dead. The head came out, and the next thing I knew, the body, up to the back hips, slithered out of her, on top of me. I was laying in the field with a baby calf covering my entire body. His head in my arms, on my chest.

He was covered in white goo ... the sac, and staring at me like I was an insane person. Which, let's face it. I was. He gasped his first breath, and Buttercup flopped her head to the ground. I got up, pulled the rest of the calf out, and Buttercup lugged herself onto all fours. She was licking and grunting at him. And me. I guess she figured since I smelled like her baby, I needed some cleaning, too.

Another thing about a cow...their tongues are a slab of muscle covering in 10 grit wet sandpaper. Very strong. And exfoliating. I rubbed the calf, shooing the flies, and she cleaned.

And then it happened. A true adrenaline rush. I was shaking from head to toe, and crying with pride and amazement. I called the vet, and we both squealed in delight. I called Jasen, and I'm still thinking he doesn't believe me. I just kept talking to Grace. A play-by-play I tell everyone I see. Partially because I'm so proud of myself I just can't stand it, and partially because I still can't believe I did it. I even called Jasen's dad.

I sat in the field, propped against a tree, for hours. Helping him scramble to his feet. I helped him begin to nurse, twirling his tail like a windmill in delight. Morph from this flopping sack of goo to a dry, adorable, giant deer-like calf. Jasen estimates he weighs a good 85 pounds. Huge.

He limped a bit, but was healthy and happy. I'm thinking the limping comes from me putting so much pressure on his knees that my hands don't work today. The joints in my fingers have never worked so hard. (Three days later, and they're still not working just right. And the little man is still a little wobbly.)

I've never been nastier, but I've also never done something this disgustingly beautiful. I told everyone giving birth felt like being Wonder Woman. Seriously. We women rock. We grow a baby, and them shove them out. How awesome is that.

This was another Wonder Woman moment. I pulled an 85 pound calf out of a 1500 lb. cow. With my bare hands. I am Wonder Woman. Seriously. Wonder Woman.

Cow Poop Soup

Yep. Jasen and Juni made cow poop soup one year. It brewed and drew flies in a giant blue bucket in the garden. I thought they were nuts.

Apparently, they're not. They're organic! This year, I bought three Guinea hens to eat the bugs out of the garden. No Sevin Dust for us. It's always freaked me out anyway.

And I used to call Jasen a cheap-ass when it came to taking care of the cows. He wouldn't buy them grain. He bought cheap hay that wasn't fertilized. We didn't fertilize or spray our fields, or spray the cows for flies.

Well, come to find out, my Redneck Husband is on the cutting edge. Grain-feed beef apparently is all the rage. Who knew?

Even cow poop soup is in style. Too bad it smells exactly as it sounds.

Crying Cows

Cows are amazing, sweet, docile creatures. In the winter, while they chew their hay, I like to close my eyes, smell the hay and listen. It's peaceful. And sounds surprisingly like water lapping against a bulkhead.

We raise gelbeigh cows. They're a large, sweet breed with a tuft of curly hair right in between their ears and large, dark eyes.

Occasionally I'll peek out my window and cuss those sweet

creatures for romping across my back yard, chomping my garden or stomping holes in the yard. But they rarely escape, and it's usually the calves that find their way out.

One day we rounded up 12 of our 18 cattle and took them to the market. It took three strong and one 85-year-old wise man, Jasen's grandfather Buddy, to load them into the stock trailers. Cows don't like to be rushed. They don't like change. And they're not stupid. Humane slaughter houses build a maze of walls leading to the end. Otherwise, the cows will refuse to move forward.

Our cows will go anywhere there's grain, since they are mostly pasture-fed. When it was all over, we had one man headed to the hospital for a suspected (but luckily not) broken hand, an exhausted 85-year-old, my redneck husband covered in cow crap, and his brother looking at a two-hour drive to the market and back.

Most of our cows will face slaughter. A few of the bulls will go on to wonderful lives as breeding stock, and maybe one or two of the young female calves will join them. But for the most part, by the time they leave our pasture, they're past their prime and have trouble keeping their weight. Some of them can be a pretty sorry sight after 15 years of bearing a calf every 15 months.

The day the cows leave doesn't bother me. I don't name the ones that will leave. I name the ones that stay. Buttercup will always stay. I can't find anyone who knows the natural life expectancy of a cow. I'm assuming that's because no one is insane enough to keep a cow as a pet. But I don't care.

It's the night after the cows leave. One of the female cows had her calf leave, and one of the calves we kept lost its mother. And they cry. Nonstop. For at least three days. They only time they stop calling for their mothers and babies is while they eat. Which means they woke me up at 3 a.m. last night, crying outside my bedroom window.

This morning, their cries were a little less loud. That's because their throats become sore from strain. Tonight, they sound like a robotic version of themselves. Their voice wanes in and out. And by tomorrow morning, half of their cries will come out silent. But still, they cry.

Daisy's calf died a few weeks after its birth last spring. It's not unusual, but heartbreaking. She nudged it, sniffed it, pawed at it with her hooves. She cried to it for a day, until Jasen came home from work to haul it into the woods. Daisy charged the ATV, and he had to whack her between her horns with a shovel. He wasn't trying to be mean, but let's face it...a charging half-ton cow with horns is not exactly easy to handle. She shook her head, and kept running after her calf. But she couldn't keep up. Her utters were too full of milk, and she stopped about 10 yards from the gate. She stood there for almost two days, crying for her calf. Searching for a way into the woods.

People tell me I give my animals human emotions that they can't possess. But I don't know. It seems very human to me to cry for a lost baby. It seems very human to me to mourn for a lost loved one. And it seems very human to me to fear the unknown and to sense death.

I feel more pain for my animals because I assign these human emotions. But I think I also find more joy in them as well. And I know we can't keep every cow or save every calf or house every stray. But for the ones we do keep, it's a pretty good life. Especially when they break into the young fall garden.

Girl POWER

DISCLAIMER: This story is surely about girl power.

Overcoming what appears too difficult to attempt. Women kicking

ass and getting it done. But...it is also about delivering a dead calf.

It's gruesome, gory and not for everyone. But it's part of being a

Redneck's wife. For those of you who choose to read, enjoy. For

those of you who skip, I don't blame you. I wish I could get the

images out of my mind.

Our cows deliver one calf each year with no problem. We

have the occasional calf die, but that's nature. Yesterday I came

home to find a cow trying to deliver her first calf. I decided to record

it. That's one tape I'll be rewinding and recording over.

She pushed for about 45 minutes, and I decided to call Jasen

over. Much more than an hour of labor will kill a calf. The hooves

were barely visible, and the cow wouldn't lay down in one spot for

more than a few contractions. We decided to lead her into the pen,

and try to help.

Helping a cow deliver is not easy. It's slippery, and hot, and

sometimes needs a come-a-long. Jasen put his hands inside of her,

grabbed onto the hooves, and pulled. Nothing. Except that he

seriously pissed off the cow. She bolted, kicked sideways and thrust

her lowered head at Jasen. Not good. We tried that route a few more times, and decided to let nature take its course. It was after hours for the vet. And like I said, we rarely have problems with deliveries. I figured we'd go back out, and everything would be over.

Two hours later, at 9 p.m., Juni was snoring in his bed, and Jasen and I were again at the barn. I'm in my nightshirt and Birks, Jasen in his underwear and coveralls. With a flashlight. And lots of bugs. My job was to shine the light at the cow's whowho, while Jasen tried to put the rope around the hooves and pull. Nothing doing. Except that we both needed showers afterward. At 11 p.m. we decided to again let nature take its course. The cow was soaked with sweat, breathing rhythmically, and pissed. But she was eating and drinking. We knew the calf was dead. It had been too long. But cows aren't like humans...it takes weeks for infection to set in. I'd hoped she'd pass it during the night.

The next morning we checked at 6 a.m. The cow was in the same standing position, and in the same ornery mood as the night before. Jasen went to work and I called the vet.

I didn't know what to expect, other than a fight with this cow. The vet arrived at 10 a.m., and got out of the truck. First of all, it was a she. About 5'8 and maybe 130 lbs. And absolutely beautiful. She had an assistant. Also a woman, and shorter than me.

So I'm thinking this is a lost cause. We don't have a shoot for the cow's head. We have three women in 95-degree heat. And a very uncomfortable, aggressive, 900 lb. cow. I'm not seeing good times ahead. I'm seeing cuts, and bruises, and heat stroke.

But within 5 minutes, the vet had roped the cow, tied her to the fence, and had an extra gate shoving her into the corner. Unbelievable. And just the beginning. She slipped her arm, up to her pit, inside and said "Holy shit. Holy shit! The calf is absolutely huge! I mean, seriously gigantic."

There was no way the calf would have been delivered without a C-section. And at this point, there was no way the calf was coming out whole.

At first I started to cry at the thought of butchering a calf before its birth. But then I remembered...it was already dead. And this was the least invasive way to save the cow.

The vet and her assistant began by threading a wire inside, wrapping it around the neck, and working the wire back and forth. The vet kept her arm inside, holding the body in place. She used every ounce of her weight to keep the cow stationary.

Twenty minutes later the vet put both arms inside, dug her boots into the concrete, and pulled with every muscle of her body. The cow squirmed, but didn't make a sound. And then it came.

A head. The whole head. And nothing but a head.

I didn't realize they were severing the neck. I also didn't realize that was just the beginning.

The vet said by the look of the body, the calf died before labor began.

The cow relaxed after the pressure of the head was removed. She relaxed, and peed. Gallons. The urine came gushing out in spurts. As did the poop. And amniotic fluid. On the vet. She took a sip of water and kept working.

She took out each front leg. The lungs and heart. The sternum. Each half of the ribcage. Each hind leg. And the placenta. Piece by piece, goo by goo, hour by hour. At 1 p.m., three hours after we began, the calf was out, the buzzards were circling, and the vet was covered, head to toe, with innards and sweat.

The hair on her arms was matted with feces. She had placenta dripping from her clothes and hands. Her boots were soaked through with urine, fluid and diarrhea. Sweat dripped from her nose. And her hair was perfect, tousled on top of her head.

Through the entire ordeal, I was half horrified by what we were doing. And half amazed at the power these women held. Their muscles bulged. They didn't give up. They said they can do anything that they put their mind to. They used leverage instead of strength. And they smiled the entire time. Pure determination.

From what we can tell, the calf weighed a good 100 lbs. The average size of our calves is 50 lbs. The vet said it was the largest calf from a grass-fed cow she'd ever seen. And it sat in a pond of its fluid, waiting for Jasen to bury it. I was too tired, too drenched with sweat, and too emotional.

It didn't bother me, taking out the calf. It's how the cow acted afterward. She wouldn't leave. She sniffed the pieces in confusion. A blur of instinct, and no baby to nurse.

The vet finally had to take a board to her head. Repeatedly. And finally, she slowly walked away, across the barnyard, and into the pasture. She didn't understand. She was soon grazing, like nothing ever happened. We pumped her full of antibiotics to deter infection, and medication to stimulate contractions to flush her system.

The vet's clothes were soaked through to her skin. She showered with the hose in our barn, scrubbing her arms with a wire-bristled brush. Then she drove off to her next appointment. It still amazes me that I was her first stop of the day.

C-sections, from what the vet said, are common in cows now. The bigger the calf, the bigger the profit. That's not for me. I want healthy, happy cows in my field.

I know this was a freak accident. Odds are it will never happen again. And I'm incredibly thankful for that. There's no way I could go through that day again. It's going to be a long time before I can walk by the pen and not see visions of what happened. Smell the stench of gasses, fluids and death. Hear belches, slurps and gushes. Feel the heat and disgust.

But with each word that I type, I feel a little better. A little more cleansed. A little more energized to raise these cows the natural, caring way. Despite the hardships, I enjoy the cows. And I enjoy the physical work I didn't think I was able to do. And I enjoy knowing that my cows are happy while they're here.

Being a Redneck's Wife is difficult. It's work, in every sense of the word. And sometimes, it's downright nasty.

Donkeys do NOT Enjoy Pedicures

Donkeys are wonderful, gentle animals. I love Bud and JD very much...if they could be cats, I honestly believe they would take the offer.

With that said, donkeys are not called jackasses for nothing. They are indeed the epitome of the jackass. They're stubborn, and smart. They're strong, and tireless. Basically, they're a giant toddler.

Donkeys need diligent hoof care just like horses. Our donkeys have not had this hoof care, and definitely needed pedicures. If their hooves are not ferried every so often, they will turn into what looks like elf feet, and it can become painful.

It took me almost two years to find a farrier to work on donkeys. Most larger businesses refuse to work on donkeys because, unlike a horse, they kick to intentionally injure the farrier. They're faster, they tend to bite more, and they're smarter. Not a safe combination. Like I said … they're jackasses.

I found a young guy, just starting out, who hadn't been hurt enough to refuse Bud and JD.

The first time he worked on the donkeys it took almost four hours, with my husband holding them. At one point the farrier had a rope wrapped around both him and the donkey, and was holding onto his back leg for dear life. This guy wrestled with that donkey for 45 minutes before he took the first snip at his hooves.

It was terrifying, and amazing at the same time. He never shouted, never hit, and never gave up.

Today was a different story. We sedated the older, ungelded donkey. He doesn't like anyone near the family jewels, and I can't blame him. But that makes it incredibly dangerous to work on his hind legs.

Apparently, donkeys have a unique gift ... they can ignore sedation and fight back. We dosed him again, and tied him to a cemented pole. He reared up, struck his hind legs toward the farrier, and clawed his front hooves up and over the fence. He snorted, even growled. Sweat began dripping off the donkey's body, down the farrier's nose, and beaded my upper lip.

It was a good 90 degrees, and painfully humid. The farrier hoisted Bud's front left hoof up under his body. That didn't work. He led him in circles and retied him to the post. That's didn't work. He had me hold him. Nope. Nothing. So we gave up.

With the smaller, younger gelding, we opted out of the sedation, because when he was castrated he had an adverse reaction. Last time JD fought for a while, but eventually submitted. This time he knew better and refused.

I'd never had to twitch an animal before. Until today. The apparatus was too large, since it's made for horses. So I had to use my hands. Try to picture this:

Grabbing a donkey's upper lip with my right hand, and twisting. Then grabbing the lower lip with my left hand, and twisting. Then, when they rare back, I don't let go. It was horrible. he was completely pissed, and just didn't give in. I let go instead of hurting him.

My options are basically to let them be (and possibly have pain in their hooves), sell or give them away to be someone else's problem (although they are very sweet, this whole farrier thing is a pain) or to have a vet come out and sedate them to the ground, which is several hundred dollars per animal. Ouch. I haven't decided what to do yet, since all of those options just plain suck to me.

Right now the farrier is licking his pride wounds, and I'm looking at the rope burn on my left hand and wondering just how sore my body will feel tomorrow.

The second we let the donkey's back into the field that night they ran to the opposite fence, pouted for 30 seconds, and then ran back to me like nothing had happened. That's my definition of a Jackass.

Is it Too Much to Ask to NOT Have Two Dead Cows in the Backyard? apparently....yes...

We have about 15 cows. It keeps the land under agricultural use, so we can afford the taxes. My husband's grandfather, has always taken care of the cows. But he's getting older, and showing the beginning effects of Alzheimer's Disease. He turned 85 in 2009. By 2015 both Buddy and his wife Nanny had passed from Alzheimer's.

Keeping the cows fed, the weeds in the fields down and the fences up is work enough. But every so often a calf dies. Here is the latest story...

One of the older cows gave birth to an unusually small calf. It seemed healthy, but very small. The mother looked horrible after the birth ... skin and bones. There's not much we can do except give the mother extra hay, unless one of us had time to bottle-feed the baby. I've done this before. It's not fun. It's literally equivalent to taking care of a newborn, and with a toddler and husband working 12-hour days seven days a week, I just didn't have time.

So the calf died three days ago. I didn't know it until I saw it half-buried in the hay barn. Buddy originally said he pulled it there out of the field, but then totally forgot all about it. He forgot the calf had died. So two days after it died, I found it. With Juni.

Anyway, I told Buddy about the calf. Five minutes later he'd forget. So I showed him the calf, had him get the tractor, and pull it out of the barn. He promised me he'd take it to the woods, where Jasen could later bury it. So I didn't think any more about it. Until the next day.

I needed to worm the cows, since Buddy obviously wasn't going to do it. I had Juni in the buggy, and the medicine with me. Then I saw it...the mother. Dead. With her head on top of her dead calf, which was still in the field. It was horrible. She'd died, still trying to get her calf to stand.

So I wormed the cows, which is not easy, and left. That night Jasen got home and I told him about it. He was so stressed from work, but seriously...two dead cows? No way can I take care of that myself, and Buddy was in no condition. So it was up to me to either hire someone, which Jasen vehemently opposed, or for him to suck it up and do it himself. He was NOT happy about the situation., but did it anyway.

Here's my take on the situation: yes, Jasen is working like crazy, and yes, I need to step up and do as much as possible. But there are some responsibilities that he just has to take care of, despite the situation at work. Two dead cows in the backyard is definitely one of them in my book.

My husband has a Girlfriend...

And she's a real heifer. Seriously. A cow. My husband is totally and completely in love with our pet milk cow, Cream. He milks her every evening, and a few weeks ago I caught him cooing to her. He brushes her, rubs her, scratches her. And she loves him right back. His truck pulls into the driveway and Cream, giant milk bag and all, clumsily runs to the gate to greet him.

We began milking Cream about a month after she had her calf, Sirloin. Hand milking is a unique experience. Cream is completely tame, so we don't hobble her, tie her up, or put her in a milking pen. We simply give her some food, and she chews contently while we milk. We didn't want to use a mechanical milker because of the cost, and the loss of connection to her comfort level. We wouldn't be able to tell if she was in pain.

Before Cream delivered her calf, Jasen told me he knew how to milk a cow. I figured as much. But here's the thing...he learned from his 87-year-old grandfather. They used hot water to clean the udders and no lube. I nursed my son for 16 months, and this method seemed totally unacceptable. Water is not a chapped nipple's friend.

I couldn't get Jasen to understand why we needed to spend money on teat wipes and Udder Butter. Until I made a very poignant comparison. "How would it feel to have someone tug on a very sensitive part of your anatomy with scratchy, dry hands for 30 minutes? Think about it for a minute, honey. Seriously." His response? "Ahhhh! Stop! I don't even want to think about it! Okay ...

I get it. Order it all tomorrow."

So now we spend the first few minutes loving on her, relaxing her and making sure she doesn't have any ticks or cuts that may hurt her. Jasen uses the wipes to meticulous clean her udders, and then lubes his hands and her udders with the cream.

The smell is glorious. It's a mixture of butter, milk, hay and comfort. And Jasen's hands are crazy soft, for the first time in his life. Added bonus!

Sometimes Cream becomes so engorged that milk squirts to the earth every time she takes a step. This drives Jasen insane. He can't stand to waste a single drop of her milk, because we all work so hard to get it.

Usually Cream stands still for us, and Jasen gets a half-gallon each day. It takes about 30 minutes, start to finish. He scoots his bucket next to her, and places his head in the soft fur where her hind legs meets her bulbous belly. He listens to the chorus of her intestines while Cream closes her eyes and chews, completely content.

But here's the thing. If Cream gets too relaxed and happy, she pees. I can strain out hair, dander, bugs, dirt. But there's no straining out urine. Each time she lifts her tail and bows her back, my job is to yell "pee!" at the top of my lungs before the golden shower hits my husband.

The other night Cream just would not move her leg, so Jasen milked her from behind. Juni whispers to me "Mommy...what if Cream pees on Daddy's head?" Just then, she lifted her tail and bowed her back. All I could yell was "Ahhhhhh....ppppppppp" before gallons of urine splashed to the floor.

The Redneck Husband deserves some credit...he's no pro athlete, but damn if he isn't quick to react. He lurched back three feet, milk bucket upright, his head unscathed from pee.

Watching Jasen milk the cow is hilarious. We don't trim or tie her tail, because we don't want her defenseless from the flies. That leaves Jasen taking whips to the cheek nightly. Every so often he milks her a little too excitedly, or a bug will irritate her tummy. That's when Jasen jumps backward before he takes a hoof to the head. She doesn't kick out of anger, but aggravation. She doesn't aim, like an unfortunate incident when Jasen tried to milk Buttercup (yes, Jim Beam helped), but simply raises her leg to let us know to knock whatever we're doing off. She doesn't have a mean bone in her body.

Last night we were all three at our wits' end. Cream wouldn't stop kicking, Jasen was exhausted from dodging her hooves, and I couldn't figure out how to calm her.

Jasen finally laid on the ground and looked under her bag (the place where the milk enters the udders). He saw giant horseflies relentlessly biting a spot the size of a nickel. Apparently, Cream injured the spot, and the flies took hold. We sprayed iodine on the area, and she immediately calmed down and stopped kicking. Sweet, sweet Cream. Jasen and I just love her gentle nature.

Milking Cream the Cow takes time. Straining and skimming the milk takes time. And then there's what to do with it all. The cream, churned into butter and buttermilk. Ice cream. Cheese. Yogurt. Jasen continuously experiments.

The raw milk tastes completely different than store bought. It's a full, round, complete taste. I prefer mine completely skimmed, since whole milk from a Jersey contains 5.5-6 % fat (store whole milk is 4%). But that skim milk is more thick, creamy and delectable than the most expensive, organic whole milk from the store.

I'm a bit lactose intolerant, so the cultures in Cream's milk helps with my digestion. Pasteurization is a wonderful invention, but it kills the bad and good bacteria. As long as we continue our meticulous treatment of Cream and her milk, no outside bacteria should enter the bottles. So far, we've experienced nothing but amazing, fresh milk.

Jasen may have a girlfriend that is out of my league ... how can I compete with four tits and fresh milk ... but she's given him a hobby, me a sense of connection to the earth and my food source, and Juni an education about where his food comes from that I could never explain with words.

I can see Cream grazing out of my office window now. It's a beautiful, sunny day, and she's a beautifully fat, happy cow. Her calf is asleep in the sun. And we have a fridge filled with jugs of milk and cream, a crock full of butter, and a sinful batch of chocolate chip ice cream in the freezer. It doesn't get more beautiful.

ok...

Our beloved Cream died in 2017. She was about 10 years old. We'd dug her out of the ditch one night, about 2 weeks after she delivered a calf. The next morning, she was dead and I was left bottle-feeding a young calf for a month. I still miss milking her.

Passing of the Cow's Guard

Jasen's grandfather Buddy raised cows on our land since he bought it in the 1960s. Even in his eighties, watching him operate the tractor was like waiting for a train wreck. Jasen rigged the tractor so it won't start. I grew tired of constantly looking out the window, waiting to see the tractor running across the field, Buddy laying in a ditch.

Buddy came out daily to feed the hungry beasts well into his eighties, but occasionally he would forget. I know this because we arrived home to find every single cow standing in our back yard, tromping their tons of weight into the saturated ground, splattering pies as they ate and leaving behind ankle-breaking holes.

It's important to note here that I love the cows. They relax me. But I'll get to that in a moment. Jasen, on the other hand, despises them. The fences, the feeding, the babies. And most of all, the escapes.

This time, they might as well have eaten cash out of his money clip. They devoured an entire bale of hydromulch, and a bag of rye seed after bursting through the barbed-wire fence protecting

Jasen's new barn addition. Pissed does not begin to describe my husband.

Sadie the Australian Shepard rounded up the cows and had them waiting at the red gate within minutes. But the damage was done. I was donned the new caretaker of the cows. And I've got to say, I don't mind.

As long as I have a decent pitch fork and tractor, the cows relax me. Here's why:

1. Feeding them in the winter is like meditation. They don't chew...they grind their food. Which sounds like water lapping upon a bulkhead. I lay on top of a roll and just listen. And then they begin to digest. Burps from stomachs one and two aren't so bad. But when they reach three and four, it gets a little hairy. And by hairy, I mean smelly. Then they begin to pee and poop. On each other. While they eat. Time for me to jet at that point.

2. The hay smells wonderful. Fresh and comforting. And when we serve peanut hay, the raw peanuts are an awesome snack.

3. A cow looks like a deer. Especially the young ones. They're sweet, and kind, and stupid beyond belief. The bull has eyes that bulge from his eye sockets. That freaks me out a bit, but Big

John isn't so bad. He also isn't full grown just yet, so we'll see if I feel the same about him in a few years. The calves hide behind their mothers, or nurse while they eat. I love how they wag their tails like a windmill and lift their heads, milk drooling from the sides of their mouths, froth dripping from their noses.

4. Cows pick their noses. With their tongues. Gross, but cool. And cute when it's a calf.

5. Cows give birth without much of a fuss. It amazes me. I've seen several from start to finish. With Daisy's first calf, I saw her contracting in the field (arching her back. And standing away from the herd) and she followed me into the pen we had at the barn. I spread out straw, and she paced. With two little black hooves sticking out and kicking. Insane. Then she laid down, hmphed with each push, and 25 minutes later had her little calf, which I named HotRod. She was exhausted and clueless, so I freed him from the sack, cleaned his nose, helped him up and watched him try to nurse. Unfortunately, she didn't have enough milk. So I bottle fed that calf for three months. One half-gallon every three hours until her mild came in. Insane! Her milk is wonderful now. She has a healthy bull calf in the field, and he's huge for his age. He can't stay, because

cows are just so stupid they'll breed their mothers. I'm not a fan of line breeding. But he's adorable while he's here. And feisty as hell.

6. It's carrying on Buddy's tradition. I love Buddy. And he loves the cows. He'll stand at the pasture, watching them eat. So do I. After dinner, I go outside, and they slowly wander to the fence, sniffing and bowing their heads, trying to figure out just what I'm doing.

And honestly, what I'm doing is paying tribute. They're wonderful animals. And they deserve respect. They feed us. And my son realizes that. It's important to understand where the grocery store comes from. The earth and the animals. We personally don't eat our cows...they have names. And I don't eat things that I name. But they will eventually be on some one's plate. Until then, they're my pets. They're spoiled. And they're food for my soul.

Sirloin Antics

Calves are awesome. So cute. So curious. So very mischievous. Sirloin was my first attempt at taming a calf.

I know what you're thinking. I'll get too attached. But I've been through this before. I bottle-fed HotRod for four months, and once he hit puberty, I was more than happy to ship him off and get my check. They turn into ... well ... the equivalent to a human 15-year-old boy. But worse. Let me digress for a moment and describe our bull, Big John, at the moment...

He waits by the gate all night for Cream to come into the pasture. (He's waiting to smell the I-can-get-preggers hormone) He spends his days strolling from ass to ass, sniffing and waiting. Pitiful.

His curly hair on top of his head is frizzy, and covered in a mud-colored substance. Key words here are mud and colored. Of course it's not mud. That would be just disgusting. It's poop. That's right. He's completely and utterly disgusting.

He doesn't mind the poop. Why, do you ask? Because it's an unfortunate risk he takes when detecting the I-can-get-preggers hormone. Which he detects by ... wait for it ... smelling and drinking the golden shower. He even scrunches his nose up to get an even better whiff. It is the most disgusting thing you will ever witness. And Jasen thinks this cow has it made. A harem of heifers.

He does what every 15-year-old boy does. By himself. (Infer here, please. I'm trying to maintain my ladylike impression). Except

Big John can just do it into thin air. It's horrible. He's a walking ton-of-disgust.

He's a wuss, but not before putting on a big show. Pawing at the dirt with his gigantic hooves. Bowing his head and thrusting it forward at me...all to deter me from getting near his ladies. Of course all I do is throw my hands in the air and he high-tails it into the middle of the field.

That is what my precious little Sirloin will become in 12 short months. A poop-wearing, piss-drinking, pleasing-himself hormone-stuffed moron.

So for now, I'm practicing with Sirloin, so when Cream does have a female, I can groom her personality like her mommy's.

One day I hit pay dirt. He now eats out of my hand. And lets me relax in the field with him. And he's just too curious. Serious. He's too curious. Licking my jeans. Licking my arms. Licking my forehead. And, what earned him a pop on his cute little nose, EATING MY HAIR. Apparently, my hair looks worse than I thought. It looks like hay. Just what I need. Less hay-like hair on my head.

He then proceeded to pout. In the chicken coup. Disgusting

already. But cute as can be.

The day the sheep kicked my bootie. And leg. And arm. And skull.

When I think of sheep, the cute, giant cotton-ball image comes to my mind. Little did I know, there exists what's called a hair sheep. They're tall, like a goat, thin and fast. Very fast. They're also pretty aggressively mean, in my opinion.

Sadie, my sweet yet inept Aussie, needed herding lessons. Bad. She herds the chickens into the pond, kids around the front yard, the guineas into the woods next door, and the cows back and forth through the pasture.

I took her to a local trainer. Apparently, my Sadie is a herding genius. I, on the other hand, need some work. A lot of work.

The trainer placed herself, Sadie, and three hair sheep in a small round pen to try out her natural instincts. She began herding them like it was her job. Instinctively picking up on the trainer's signals, and running those sheep like it was her job.

Am I sexy, or what? My vote is what.

My job was to simply walk across the ring and exit through

the metal gate. The trainer said that if the sheep headed my way, to simply throw my hands in the air and they'll divert. It did not go well.

The first time they ran toward me, I threw my hands up and they scatter in the opposite direction. The second time they charge I raised my hands, and no such luck. I was backed against a 6-foot metal fence. And they ran UP me. Not around. Not over. UP.

I felt six front hooves dig into my leg. Then my forearms. They my forehead. I stumbled into the center of the ring, dazed and seriously confused. And crying behind my sunglasses because I was just that embarrassed. It was kickball in fifth grade all over again. I'd gotten smacked, and it hurt my body and pride.

The people watching rushed to open the gate, grab water, and Advil. Lots of Advil. Once I got over the initial shock, I realized just how beat up I was. My head pounded. I was bleeding. And I was sleepy.

I don't consider myself graceful. I'm always finding mysterious bruises from run ins with random tables, chairs and animals. But this time, the sheep kicked my bootie. And leg. And arm. And skull. One for the records. Saide never learned how to truly herd. She spends her days napping and occasionally tormenting the cows. When we need to herd them, we lock Sadie in the barn because it's just easier that way.

They Call them Birdbrains for a Reason

We've raised many birds over the years. Chickens. Geese. Ducks. And now guineas.

And let me tell you...they're all stupid. The ducks were afraid of water. The geese landed on the barn while learning to fly. Once, one of the chickens drowned in their own water bowl. And it takes the guinea's two hours to find their way out of their coops. If one is left in our out, it rams its chest against the chicken wire, not thinking to walk around to the door.

I may not have the most commonsense in the world. I count on my fingers. I can't do multiplication in my head. And I can't do percentages, even when armed with a calculator.

But so far I haven't drowned in my bathtub (except for the time when Jasen caught me passing out in the tub from Benadryl to get rid of the hives throwing my Dad's 50th birthday party gave me), I can find my way out of my house (although I can't find my key to get back in) and I can back my car out of the driveway (except for the time I couldn't, and plopped into the ditch, and had to get Jasen to yank me out).

But the next time someone calls me a birdbrain, I'm going to kick their ass. Them's fightin' words, I tell you. Fightin' words. These are to quote my husband. I would never say that.

Chapter 5: Stuff that Doesn't Fit Anywhere else

Sometimes the Redneck Husband just does shit. Here are the gems that just don't quite fit anywhere else.

If you Pee there I will Seriously Kill You

My Redneck Husband likes his beer. Every night, he likes his beer. He's definitely a self-described functioning alcoholic. He uses it to relax; take away the stress. I used to argue with him about it, but, at least in the beginning of our marriage, reluctantly accepted the drinking.

My husband used to drink brown liquor like it was Kool Aid. But it changes him. He becomes a complete asshole. Flirty and funny with everyone else, a complete asshole to his wife.

He asks me if he can have a few brown liquor drinks every now and then. This particular night, we were at a New Year's party with my dad and his wife, and a very large man with a very large tolerance for all things alcoholic.

Apparently, my husband and the large man started talking, and of course drinking. Let me make something perfectly clear: A Redneck can hold his liquor. In his drinking heyday, I'm sure he could keep pace with the best of them. But after a few years of a beer-only diet, his body doesn't handle the rough stuff like it used to.

We had a great time at the party, and my husband never showed his evil side that only comes out after a night with Jim Beam. Once we got home I put on the t.v. and he passed out on the couch.

Or so I thought.

Twenty minutes later, my husband rises. His skin was that pale, green, clammy color people get when they're drop-down drunk or coming down with the flu. Apparently his bladder woke him up. He told me he had to pee.

Since he said he had to pee, I thought it odd that he didn't take his post on our front porch, as was his usually peeing preference. And yes, I feel bad for our neighbors when he whips it out without warning. But they're old and can't see that well, and I digress.

It was odd, because instead of passing through the kitchen on his way to the bathroom, he stopped at the refrigerator first. Did he really need a snack for the bathroom? Nope. He opened the bottom veggie drawer, and I heard his zipper.

"What the hell are you doing? That is NOT a bathroom. That's the refrigerator you jackass! If you pee there, I will seriously kill you..."

He stumbled around, and shut the refrigerator door. And then I heard it. That sound of pee hitting something that obviously was not the toilet. It was the outside of our $200 stainless steel trashcan we'd bought the week before. The trashcan he insisted we needed. The trashcan that was now covered in Jim Beam-laden urine.

And there was my husband, in all his redneck glory, jeans around his ankles, eyes glossy and completely unconscious to the world around him. He slept on the couch that night, and was not at all pleased about the mess all over the kitchen. He had no recollection.

He also spent the next hour apologizing for defacing our kitchen, and cleaning his prized trash can.

The Whole World is his Toilet

My Redneck husband isn't a bathroom kind of guy – can you tell yet? He believes in the great outdoors. He believes in feeling the elements while he does his business. He believes the whole world is his toilet.

My sister, her now ex-husband (whom at the time was her boyfriend), my dad, my husband and I met for dinner one night at a local restaurant/bar. I desperately wanted my Dad to like my husband. This night definitely helped. It defies all logic, but believe it or not, the two most important men in my life bonded over poo.

Talk of poo, gas and other tummy problems is always commonplace in my family. We call it the "Thrasher Family Belly." It's disgusting, I know, but it's my family. My dad has an especially severe case of Thrasher Belly, second only to his father. I finish a very close third, but that's beside the point.

This particular night my husband and my Dad stuffed themselves into oblivion at dinner. And then it happened...the

Redneck Husband got a case of the Thrasher Belly. But apparently, he didn't feel comfortable doing said issue in the public bathroom.

Instead, my Redneck Husband felt much more comfortable in the bushes. The bushes outside. Beside the restaurant. In an elderly woman's back yard. Nice fertilizer, I guess.

I was mortified. It was then that I found his secret stash of toilet paper in his truck, kept conveniently hidden for just such emergencies. Even now, he frequently squats beside a tractor, behind a truck door or somewhere in the woods...all while on a job site.

Lucky for me, my Dad finally felt comfortable around my husband from this moment on. He'd joined the Thrasher Family Belly club, and took it to a new, if more disgusting, level. Our dinner discussions temporarily took a more subdued tone while my Dad dated his wife, but since they've been married the poo talk is back up and running.

What in God's Name is the SOUND?

I do not throw up. Okay, wait. That's not entirely true. I've thrown up once in the past 25 years. I had a stomach bug a few years ago. But, I did manage to make it through my 21st birthday, sick as a dog, rocking back and forth and not throwing up for three days. Not an ounce. I made it through pregnancy, dry-heaving for months, lurching over the toilet, toting my big blue plastic bowl around the house. Nothing. I even made it through Juni's projectile vomit without one drop of sympathy puke.

I will pray to whatever power will listen to not throw up. I'll sweat, cry, plead, and beg. I realize no one enjoys throwing up. But I absolutely despise it. \

Jasen, as in basically other aspect of our lives, is the polar opposite. No, he does not enjoy throwing up, but he'll take a good Pukefest over feeling the least bit queasy. A bit too much Jack Daniels and he's on the front steps, leaving his dinner for the dogs. A steak he let get a little too green and he's on the back porch fertilizing the roses. Stomach bug? Not for long. You get the picture.

I don't mind it when Jasen loses his lunch outside. It's when he's inside that there's an issue. This night proved a classic example.

My Dad prepared his absolutely delicious mussels in wine and butter broth. Tasty does not begin to describe this dish. Jasen had not so much as swallowed a single mussel for about eight years, since the last time my dad made them. That time, he used butter. A lot of butter. I'd venture to guess Jasen ate a good pound of mussels. And an even better pound of butter. Later that night, he puked a good pound of mussels, and an even better pound of butter. After the other night, I'm thinking Jasen is allergic to mussels.

I've reached my un-scientific diagnosis because this time was different. There was very little butter. They were delicious in every way. My stomach welcomed every tasty bit of shellfish delight.

So imagine my surprise when I hear Jasen puking at 2 am. Everyone's husband pukes. I realize this. But here's what makes mine different:

When Jasen really has a good puke, it lasts for hours. Two, in this particular instance. Two hours of puking. Two hours of torture for him, and me.

And here's why it's torture for me. The sound in insane. There are no words to describe. But I'll try. The volume jolts me out of a dead sleep. Even a Xanax-induced sleep. Granted, I'm a light sleeper, but this sound causes me to sit straight up in bed, terrified there's an earth quake. Or some sort of alien invasion. Or an airplane headed straight for the front yard.

It's like he's puking from his pancreas. Hoo-waa, Hoo-waa...similar to Al Pacino in Scent of a Woman. Only in a demonic voice. I've witnessed the event with my eyes only once. It freaked me out so bad I'll never walk in again. He pukes with his entire body. Muscles I didn't think he had bulging. His hair on end. His face tomato-red. I asked him once why he was so violent with the event. I thought maybe he had some sort of exotic disease that caused his puking mechanism to go haywire.

"I want to get it all out. When I'm pukin', I'm not playin'. You sit there crying over the toilet. I'm not into that. I want that shit out, man. You gotta just get the shit out."

Gotcha. So he's forcing the contents of every internal organ out through his mouth. I get it. The other night, I drifted in and out of sleep after asking him if he needed anything and he replied "ugh...hoo-waa...no, babe...hoo-waa. I'm fine. Don't come it. Fucking mussels. I'm never touching fucking mussels again in my life. hooooo-waa." Flush.

Here are some other choice phrases that woke me up.

"Oh, my God. I though mussels smelled bad before they were digested."

"These fuckers taste fucking horrible."

"Damn. Damn! Hoo-waa, hoo-waa." Flush.

"Ohhhh...lord. Hooo-waa. I have to get up in two hours. Hoo-waaaaaaa." Flush.

Apparently, he decided at some point to gargle some of my mouthwash to try and mask the taste of mussels, bile and our accompanying dish, spaghetti. Yep. Spaghetti. Everyone's favorite food to expel. the mouthwash was a version of Listerine meant to help whiten teeth. Which means it contains peroxide. Foaming peroxide.

"Oh holy Hell. What the Hell is in the shit? Jesus. I'd rather taste the puke. Oh God...it's drizzling down the back of my throat...Hoo-waaa. Hoooooo-waaaaa....HOOOO-WAAAA." Flush.

And then, just as abruptly as it began, it stopped. It was also the next morning. Towels from wiping his mouth were in the hamper. There was no sign of the nightmare that was the night before in the bathroom. His eyes featured circles from the lack of sleep. He bitched about the mussels ad nauseum. His skin boasted a bit of a green tint, but other than that he seemed fine. He even took out the trash he'd forgotten the night before...mussel shells and all, without missing a beat.

I hadn't realized until later that day that he'd drizzled a bit of vomit on the toilet. After Sadie licked the toilet for 30 minutes while I got ready that morning, and then gave me a love lick on my calf. Now that I realize she was licking the remnants of puke, I'm not so happy about that bit of affection.

Jasen came home that night, walking a little funny. I didn't say anything until later that night, when he got into bed.

"Umm...Honey? Is something wrong? You're not quite as frisky as usual."

"Yeah, well...I'm pretty sure I pulled something last night while I was puking."

"Pulled something?"

"Yeah. I'm seriously never eating mussels again. Don't even bring them into the house. I definitely pulled something. Something important. Damnit."

"Ummm...okay...you're not giving me much to go by, here, babe."

"I think I pulled, you know, my love muscle. Is that possible?"

Oh...Good...Lord. My husband is hilarious.

The $1600 Duck

My husband owns the reputation of driving incredibly slow. I'm sure that's partly due to his vehicle - an F450 dual-wheeled, diesel, extended cab, flatbed truck. It's basically a tow truck with a full backseat. Doesn't get much slower than that. But it's also due to the fact that my husband is a tight-ass. He doesn't want to spend his money on anything intangible. Which I tend to agree with.

Jasen rarely gets speeding tickets, and I don't think he's ever had an accident. I, on the other hand, have dings along my car and have racked up a few tickets through the years.

But the $1600 hunting ticket my husband and ex-brother-in-law both received a few years back wipes the slate clean. Even at two speeding tickets a year, it'll take me a good 5 years until he can bitch. And that's not happening any time soon, especially considering the $200 I just paid for him speeding back to work last month.\

Jasen insists on keeping a gun cabinet filled with shotguns in the living room. I hardly remember it's there anymore. Neither do I think about the gun propped next to our bed. Jasen rarely shoots anything. He began to think twice about hunting after he shot a raccoon in our barn, and then noticed her babies. He came into the house that night with tears in his eyes. He'll shoot an aggressive snake or annoying bird periodically, but beyond that he's relatively docile. And I am simply not a gun person. They scare the hell out of me. And I'm fairly certain that if I ever did decide to shoot a snake on my own I'd end up with one less toe.

For whatever reason, he and a friend decided to go bird hunting one fall. Of course, neither of them thought to actually buy a hunting license. Or the federal bird stamps. Or the lead-free bullets. Or check to make sure their guns were up to code.

He and Jamie drove to a friend's farm and proceeded "to shoot at everything that flew by," as Jasen explained. They killed a few ducks, two geese, and then realized the game warden truck at the end of the dirt path near Jasen's truck. Not good.

My Redneck Husband apparently chucked his gun in the ditch and turned around. This did not please the game warden. Again, not good.

It's important at this point to explain my impression of some game wardens. They think they're badass. They're like animal control, with guns. Barney Fife would be proud.

This particular game warden decided to smack my husband with every charge he could render. Hunting without a license. Hunting without a federal duck stamp. No plug in the gun (Jasen decided to take that out for some reason), and using lead shot. Brilliant.

In addition to the charges, the game warden decided to subpoena Jasen to court. In Richmond. On a weekday. All because he chucked his gun in the ditch, and I'm sure used some choice words to describe his impression of Mr. Fife.

Jasen missed the class on temper control, so it was up to me to get him out of the court appearance. I'd rather pay the fine than pay the bail. I called the Virginia Department of Hunting and Fishing to get the whole story. The warden wrote in his report that Jasen ran from police.

Ummm...yeah. Again, something else important to note. My husband does not run. Under any circumstances. I've seen him walk through a hurricane, walk to the house when I was in labor, and walk to me when I got my finger stuck in the cheese grater.

I explained this to the prosecutor. I also explained that my husband

and brother-in-law do not possess the best judgement when together. And that he probably did give the game warden lip. And that I would punish his crime with more vigor than any judge in Richmond.

The prosecutor agreed. He signed off and allowed me to pay the fines without Jasen appearing in court.

The $1600 ticket is well worth the price. Unless I find myself in a high-speed chase with the police, it's pretty unlikely I will ever rack up enough moving violations to compete with the 45-minute hunting trip.

The ticket makes for a wonderful ace in my pocket. And with a husband like Jasen, that's priceless. And just in case you're wondering...no, we did not have duck or goose for dinner. The game warden, I'm assuming, did. I hope he chipped his tooth on a nice leaded shot.

Buying a Red Cedar Log from a transitioning Transgender Person

I consider myself an accepting, politically correct person. I teach Juni not to stare at anyone. To celebrate our differences and realize it's those differences that make this world beautiful and interesting.

So imagine my surprise when I found myself stumbling over my words and struggling to peel my eyes from a person different from me.

Jasen had lusted over a gigantic red cedar log in the front yard of a blue house on the other end of our road. I know the question...what would one do with such a log? The answer is simple, if you are a proper Redneck. You take it to your buddy, who happens to have a mobile sawmill, and make boards. Then you dry the boards for months, then you create furniture. My husband crafts some of the most amazing furniture. He's a perfectionist, so he'd argue with me, but I love what he creates. But, as usual, I digress.

I wrote down the number for the person selling the log, and called. The man who answered said his name was Julie. Okay. A little odd, but who am I to judge? Juni isn't exactly on the top 100 list of names.

We talked price, and I told him I would drop by and pay him that day. And then he kept talking. About what I'm thinking are inappropriate things for someone you've never actually met. His divorce. His kids. His job. His age.

Shit. He's going to flirt with me when I get there. Not a good situation. Especially with Juni in tow. But Jasen had his heart set, and I knew I had to suck it up, grow a pair, and knock on the blue house's door. I saw his neighbor in his yard, so I felt safe. Plus, I told my ginormous tree guy and dear friend, Dallas, where I was. Just in case.

I walked up the steps, and knocked. The door opened, and my jaw dropped. I couldn't move my eyes. I couldn't think of words, or get them out. This is not going well. Not well at all. I'm starting to sweat.

Here's what opened the door: a person towering over me at a good 6 feet tall. Man feet, without shoes or socks. The largest hands I've ever seen in my life. Larger than Jasen's, my Dad's, even Dallas'. Short, permed hair. A hot fuscia, short sleeved, mock turtleneck sweater. Makeup from 1985...we're talking blue eyeshadow, hot pink lipstick, and enough blush to cover four faces. Perfectly smooth skin.

And yes...my eyes had to check to see if there was a package. Nope. But, as my sister informed me, there is such a thing as tuck and tape. Who knew? Julie also had giant boobs. Perfect boobs. Obviously fake boobs.

Did I mention this person had the deepest voice I'd ever heard? Yep.

"Ummm...I'm looking for Julie?"

"That's me. Hold on just one sec. I'm giving my mom a perm."

"Ummm...Oh. Oh. OK."

Internal thoughts "Oh my friggin lord. This is insanity. If Jasen only knew. Oh holy Hell. Dallas has to come over here and get the log for me. Geeze. Can he handle that? Poor Dallas...such a good 'ol boy."

Juni noticed nothing but the old dog and kitty inside the house. No mention of the obviously transitioning Julie.

So I paid the money, got in my car, and dialed a close friend who was also a tree worker. He said he'd be there in 45 minutes to check out the situation.

The situation, as it turns out, is that Julie liked The Redneck Friend. A lot. His name used to be James, and he explained how he is becoming Julie. The Redneck Friend was obviously being hit on. He couldn't figure out why.

But I could...he's a tree man. And his truck's license plate says...wait for it... okay, this is so good you have to wait again... his license plate says...

LUVWOOD

Look what I caught, Babe

Our kitchen floor is constantly covered with mud, grass seed and straw from Jasen's boots. I've come to realize that a clean house just isn't in the cards for us. Dirt is inevitable in the country and his line of work.

For the first six months of our marriage I bitched and moaned every afternoon about him wearing his boots in the house. When nagging failed to do the trick, I went on strike. I didn't sweep, mop or vacuum for seven days.

I'm sure Jasen noticed, but he never said a word. I gave up and decided to end the strike but keep up the bitching. He still wears his boots in the house.

The mud reaches its peak during February and any other day that it rains. Jasen doesn't work much in the rain, so he's usually messing around at the barn or with equipment.

One rainy day in June, when our son was almost four months

old, I heard the door squeak open. I walked downstairs, hoping to stop him from waking the baby. There stands my husband, dripping wet with the bottom six inches of his jeans caked in mud.

He was balancing in the doorway, trying to keep his boots off of the white kitchen tile, holding the oldest, most rusted coffee can I have ever seen.

"Babe, come here and look what I caught," he said to me.

Okay, so I'm thinking there is no way in Hell I'm going to put my face anywhere near that can. You couldn't pay me enough at this point. For all I know there's a snake, frog or some other type of slimy creature waiting to hiss and bite at me.

He smiles mischievously and promises me there's nothing disgusting in his can. I tell him take it outside and I'll look. So here I am, peering into this coffee can, looking straight into the eyes of an extremely pissed off crawfish.

Apparently this crawfish was playing in a puddle, minding his business when Jasen decided to scoop him up, into the can. We eat crawfish all the time - it's one of our favorite special meals. Jasen wanted to show me what one of the little buggars looked like alive.

The humor of this encounter wasn't so much that Jasen

brought me a crawfish, which he subsequently put back in the puddle, but that I saw the next 10 years flash before my eyes. Once Jasen Jr. begins walking, there's no telling what he will have in that coffee can on a rainy day, smiling mischievously and saying "mom, come look what dad and I caught."

Pickled Pigs Feet

People tell me I have a heightened sense of smell. My olfactory glands must be directly connected to my memory, because smelling specific scents springs memories to mind. And I think people are correct - I think I do have a powerful sniffer.

That's a good thing. And a bad thing. It's an especially bad thing when cooking something that just down right stinks.

Such as pickled pigs feet. Let me make one thing perfectly clear. I have never, nor will I ever, dine on any sort of foot. No offense, but it just doesn't appeal to me one bit. Toe jam just isn't a flavor I'm up for experiencing.

But Jasen's grandfather Buddy loved pickled pigs feet. It's important to understand that this man lived in a home with a dirt floor when he was a child. It was during the Great Depression, and the family hid their chickens under the house so people wouldn't steal them. He ate turnips every night. Pickled pigs feet were a treat.

Pickled pigs feet are not easy to come by. I searched three grocery stores, and never found any. I did, however, find uncooked feet at Food Lion one day a few years before his death. For some reason I thought it would be a good idea to cook Buddy a big pot of pickled pigs feet.

Yes, it was a sweet idea. But smart, absolutely not. The feet take hours to pickle. And you have to skim scum off of the top of the water every few minutes. Not to mention you actually have to handle a pig's former foot.

But those issues pale in comparison to the smell. The smell singes your nose hairs. It creeps through the air, and before you know it has completely invaded your home.

The problem is that the smell invades so slowly that I didn't notice. Plus it was winter, and therefore I didn't think to open a window or door. My sister stopped by for a visit.

My sister doesn't share my olfactory gift. She does, however, possess a fairly strong gag reflex. She dry-heaved for half an hour before we went outside. Once we came back in, I dry-heaved for three days before the stink left.

I'll never cook pigs feet again. Believe it or not, Harris Teeter carries the feet pre-pickled. And so, every few weeks I pick up a jar, vow to the teenager ringing my order that I've never have and never will eat them, and surprise Buddy. He says they're not as tasty as my batch, but I'm thinking that's just too bad. My nose just can't take another pickling session with a swine's toe jam.

Up at 4:45 am because of the Fire Alarm

I despise our smoke detectors. I realize they serve a very important purpose. Jasen's childhood home burned to the ground because its renters drank a case of beer and left the grill on while they made a run to 7-11. But despite their purpose, our smoke detectors drain 9v batteries, and only beep that ear-piecing ring signaling a dead or dying battery in the middle of the night. Of course, I never remember to stock 9v batteries since the detectors are the only devices that use them, and we end up listening to the beep for half a day. I thought that was bad. Until this specific morning.

The smoke detectors went off full force. At 4:45 a.m. That's right. It was still dark outside. I woke up immediately, and gave

Jasen a swift slap to the side to wake him up. The alarms screeched for about 30 seconds and then stopped. Huh. We still can't decide if it was one or all of the alarms, but at 4:45 a.m. it not only doesn't matter where that sound is coming from, but I also did not possess the consciousness to differentiate between such possible origins.

Both of us sat straight up in bed and began to climb out just as the alarms quieted. Curious. They beep once every 10 minutes when the battery is weak. And if there was a fire, you'd think they'd scream for more than a half-minute, considering the repercussions. After a few minutes of debating its source and reason, the alarms sounded again.

This time, Jasen popped out of bed and began to walk toward the bedroom door. They stopped again. Jasen, naked as a jaybird, now stands underneath the fire alarm, his hair standing straight on end, eyes bloodshot, and the sound of his stubby fingernails dragging across his hairy legs as he scratched himself, irritating my ears like wet sandpaper to skin.

I couldn't help but laugh. It really was a sight. A sight to see, now that's debatable. But nonetheless a sight. Jasen peeked in Juni's bedroom and found him still sleeping soundly. He then tapped the guest bedroom doorknob (like they teach you in elementary school) to see if it was hot. I keep this door strategically closed because inside lays a massive disaster of crafts in progress.

The alarms kept going off every few minutes. Jasen pulled on a pair of jeans and a sweatshirt, trudges downstairs and checked every room and the outside perimeter of the house. There is definitely an absence of fire. I'm laughing so hard tears are streaming down my face when I point to the attic.

Jasen stomps outside to get the ladder, waking Juni into a terrified screaming fit. The only thing I could think to do for him was to cover his ears with my Hokies ear warmers to muffle the sound. He's now yelling "Daddy! Don't get burned in dat attic! Dem loud fings say there's a fire!"

So now Juni is wearing earmuffs and yelling about his Daddy burning in a fire, Jasen is flipping through the fire detector instruction manuals, and I'm asking if we should call the fire department. I realize there's no fire, but I also realize these alarms are hellbent on ruining my morning and I'm honestly out of options and ideas at this point.

And then the noise stops. Just like that. Crisis over. Charred remnants of house averted. The alarms blasted one more time at 8:45 a.m. and Jasen changed the batteries that afternoon. They've been silent ever since. But I still bought 16 9v batteries at Home Depot. Just in case.

Yes, honey. The Pope is a Virgin

My husband was raised Catholic. His father attended a private school, nuns with rulers smacking hands and everything. You'd think he'd know something about the religion. Not so much.

This story takes place the day The Pope announced his resignation. I made the comment that "I'd say his reasoning is to spend some time with his family. But he can't have kids. That's kind of sad, when you really think about it."

"The Pope can't have kids? Why not?"

"Are you kidding me? You're kidding me, right? Babe…the Pope is celibate. All Catholic priests are."

"What the heck does celibate mean? You do this all the time. Use big words you know I don't know."

"Ummm, yeah.   Not a big word. It means he's a virgin. He can't have sex. When Catholic priests become priests, they promise to become celibate. Personally, I think that's a problem. Remember all the reports of molestation? Some men think God will save them from being gay if they become a priest. Not so much."

My husband didn't hear anything past the word virgin. He literally sat straight up, eyes like a deer in headlights.

"You mean they can't screw? Ever?"

"No, honey, they can't. Weren't you raised Catholic? Your grandmother went to church twice a week every week of her life. The IRS audited them three times because they didn't believe anyone would donate so much money to a church. Your dad's hands were smacked with rulers. Even your mom goes to a Catholic church. And you're telling me you never realized priests are celibate? Wait. Excuse me. You never realized that priests can't...screw?"

"I don't fill my head with facts I don't need to know. Sucks for them, though."

"Babe! You're Catholic! Celibacy is one of the pillars of your religion! It's kind of important to know these things."

"They can't screw. That sucks. But I can. That's all I need to know."

Chapter 6: All Things Food

Cooking for Jasen

Despite my complete hatred over Jasen assigning me a resolution to cook more often from scratch, I decided to swallow my pride, suck it up, and I tried homemade chicken and dumplings. We're talking pastry blenders, rolling pins, the whole bit. It was beautiful. I added extra spices and veggies, and leftover chicken from my first attempt at feeding a picky husband who compliments his own cooking ad nauseum.

He gets home, and I'm helping Juni with his homework. The kitchen is immaculate. The house smells like comfort food, and I'm completely proud of myself.

He asks what's for dinner, I tell him, and he takes a peek. And the conversation begins...

Jasen "So, what does this go over? Rice? Noodles? Ohhh....egg noodles would be good."

Me: "It's chicken and dumplings. It's a one-pot meal. There's chicken, peas, carrots, corn, and dumplings. The dumplings ARE the starch."

Jasen: "Okay! I was just asking."

Me: "K."

Five minutes later...

Jasen: "How about some cornbread to go with it? That's sounds awesome! But I'll cook it. You don't know how to make cornbread like I do."

Me: Silent for 15 seconds, then "You're effing kidding me, right?"

Jasen: "I was just sayin', it would be good. But if it's going to hurt your feelings, never mind."

Me: "Of course it hurts my feelings! What did I tell you? I cook, you eat, and you don't complain. That's how this is going to go. If you complain, I don't cook, and I kill you. Got it?"

Jasen: "Why are you so mean to me? I just want some cornbread. You know what? Never mind the cornbread. I'll just eat this. This is fine."

Me: "Okay! Mommy needs a timeout. I'm going to fill Juni's tub, you wash him, and I'm taking a shower. A long one. I swear, if you knock on that bathroom door I'll ... I don't even know. Do NOT knock on that door. Seriously."

Jasen: "Damn...don't you think you're over-reacting a little?"

Me: "Babe...I love you. But you're driving me crazy."

Thirty-five minutes later. Jasen takes his shower, I have everything ready to eat when he comes downstairs, including his sweet tea.

Immediately, he douses his bowl with pepper. I manage to not yell at him for not at least trying it first. But believe me...my blood is still boiling.

Dining with the Redneck Husband

Cooking for Jasen is miserable. He hovers. He complains. He farts. I hate it. He's a better cook, and he knows it.

Dining with Jasen is an experience. Our first "experience" was at Carvers, a nice restaurant in Chesapeake. I was 15, and horrified when Jasen put a loaf of bread down his over-sized jeans instead of asking for a to go box. He is the definition of raised in a barn. I don't know who taught him manners, but they failed. Miserably.

This particular weekend we traveled to Blacksburg for the Virginia Tech game. You see, I got my undergrad degree from

Virginia Tech, and as they say, I bleed Chicago maroon and burnt orange. Go Hokies! But I digress. We stayed in Roanoke, and made reservations at the four-star Hotel Roanoke for Friday night. Hotel Roanoke is the best restaurant within 75 miles of the city. Seriously.

Going to propose? Hotel Roanoke. Graduation? Hotel Roanoke. Tech game without your six-year-old? Hotel Roanoke.

We're shown to our white-linen table, and peruse the menu. Apparently, the peanut soup is a must. To be honest, I was a bit scared to try an entire bowl, so I ordered the $3 sample. It was lovely. Creamy, with some sort of chicken or vegetable stock undertone, and chopped peanuts to top it off. It's been on the menu since 1935.

Jasen takes a sip "Jesus Christ, Frances. I can make this. Get me a jar of peanut butter, a cup of water, and some chopped peanuts. And there ya go. Peanut soup. Give me my $3 back."

Lovely. We sat and talked for a bit, and The Redneck Husband has an epiphany. He realizes the possibilities of the flask I bought him for his birthday. I ordered a peach martini, and he ordered an $8 beer.

"Babe...I just thought of the best idea ever. I take my flask into every restaurant we go to. I order a Coke, or whatever. And then I just take it to the bathroom and add the vodka."

"You're going to take your drinks into the bathroom? That's gross honey."

"It's not gross. It's going to save us a fortune...think of how much I drink at dinner. We'll save thousands!"

"Okay. Do what you want. But I'm hiding in the ladies room while you're ducking under the table to spice up your Coke."

Dinner was great. We both learned what "Pittsburg Rare" means. Not something Jasen felt up for with a sirloin. Charred on the outside, literally cold on the inside. A cold marbled steak turned off even my meat-devouring man.

After dinner Jasen immediately asked "So...where's the pisser in this place?"

I downed the remainder of my delish martini and asked for the dessert menu.

There was some chocolate concoction the waitress described as ordinary, a salted caramel cake that sounded like perfection, and Banana's Foster. I wanted caramel. Jasen wanted a sundae from Dairy Queen.

"What the fuck is Bananas Foster?"

"It's a dessert, honey. They flambé it table-side. Watch ... that man is getting it for his little boy."

"Jesus. I'll give you Bananas Foster. You get a bunch of bananas from Harris Teeter, I'll grab a blow torch from the barn and ... poof ... an $18 dessert. Hey...that kid's got a chef's hat on. I want one of those. Not for me. For Juni."

The waitress brought Jasen a chef's hat for Juni. The entire weekend, that hat sat on the console of the 4Runner because Jasen wanted it to arrive in perfect condition for our little man. He may have zero manners, but his heart makes up for it.

I ordered the caramel cake, and thanks to the waitress, the chef made Jasen a vanilla sundae to save me a trip to Dairy Queen.

My Steak and Potato Man, Hold the Potato

Steak is Jasen's favorite meal. I've known this since we were 15. Now this is not to say that Jasen doesn't like other types of food. The boy will eat anything. He could eat nails and his stomach would take it in stride.

And he'll try just about anything. He ate chitlins at my

granddaddy's party once. Granted, he tasted those chitlins for three days from indigestion and swears he'll never eat one again, but he tried them. He loves turnips. I don't like the taste of turnips or the smell of his gas after he eats them, but he grows them every year nonetheless.

He also loves sushi. My family introduced him to sushi when we were teenagers. We took him to a Japanese steakhouse, and he ordered the largest meal on the menu. He then proceeded to scarf down the remnants of my entire family's meal. We eat sushi several times a month now.

But regardless of his love for anything almost edible, his first love remains steak.

Like all new fathers, Jasen wanted his son to love the same things. Jasen Jr. wasn't more than two weeks old when my husband turned to me one night and asked straight-faced, "honey, when can Junior have steak?" I laughed, but this obviously was not as funny to Jasen. He was completely serious about the subject of feeding our infant son steak.

I explained that Jasen Jr. would drink milk for the first few months and nothing else, and then he'd start cereal. I told him that he could begin eating more solids between six and nine months, but that even then, the meat was more like mush than anything else.

Jasen was crushed. I actually caught him dabbing steak sauce on our son's lips one night when he was three months old. Starting him off right, he explained when I freaked out.

The Top 10: A Couple's Resolution

The Redneck and I made a resolution one year that we could with: Eat at the Hampton Road's Magazine's Top 10 Restaurants. Both of us love to eat. And cook. And eat some more. So why not combine eating with a relationship renewal? We decided to begin at No. 10 and work our way up.

One night we declared game on with Salacia, in the oceanfront Hilton. Here's what dining at the No. 10 restaurant is like with a partially reformed Redneck...

It began by Jasen climbing into my 4Runner with three beers down and one in hand. Twenty minutes later we're stuck in unmoving traffic headed from Chesapeake to the beach. Not exactly the best beginning with a man whom cusses at someone driving a half-mile under the speed limit.

So we ditch the interstate and opt for Shore Drive. I can't help but think about all of the fatal accidents on that road, and wonder why. Jasen decides he has to pee. Immediately. I tell him he's a 34-year-old man, and can hold it for 10 minutes. Our reservations are at 6:30 p.m. We're 15 minutes away from the Hilton. It's 6:28 p.m. You do the math, because apparently, he couldn't.

My husband cannot hold it, and so he proceeds to take my perfectly good bottle of Dasani water and dumps it out the window, preparing it for a true Redneck potty break. I will absolutely not have my husband urinate in my water bottle, in my new car. Especially after he's lost the top.

So I pull over. And he hikes it into the woods. Nice. Predictable. Hilarious, and much better than the last time we visited the Hilton for a formal event, where he peed in the parking lot. And on his suit. But I digress.

We're a bit late, but no worries. We're sat between two couples. Jasen has no idea the matre' d will place a napkin in his lap. Too funny. I'm pushing him to try the Kobe. But at $65 for a piece of meat with no sides, he's just too chicken. So cowboy steak it is. I'm up for the rockfish, since I'm still trying to lose a few pounds and really don't cook anything but salmon at the house. I, too, am a chicken every now and then.

One absolutely, perfectly indulgent martini later, and I'm a happy girl. the couple to my right receives their appetizer, and Jasen begins to lean over.

And when I say lean over, we're talking crossing the 3-foot personal space line, here.

"Whatcha got?"

"Jasen, let them eat their dinner."

"Babe! Let me talk. I wanna know what they got." I blush, and he continues. "Whatcha got? Whatya order? Whya here...what's the occasion?" Good lord. Here we go.

This lovely couple features the man in a Christmas tie, and the woman in a Christmas sweater. They're here because they have $65 in coupons. I'm looking at the menu, and wishing I had $65 in coupons.

Before I know it, the younger couple to my left has their dinner. The wife is talkative like me. Her husband, quiet, staring down, his face inches from his plate. Obviously blind. Unfortunately, not obviously blind to Jasen. Wait for that one to bite me in the ass later.

"Whatcha got? Whya here?"

"Jasen! seriously! What the hell, man?"

"Babe! I'm just making conversation!"

Again, this couple rocks. The wife actually hands Jasen a plate with a bite of creamed spinach on it. Which he later orders. They're from Connecticut. Her father has had a stroke, and they're taking a break from the hospital.

By the end of the dinner, I have shared my swordfish with her, hugged her, and told both couples about my grandparents, how Jasen and I met, and know so much about each couple I feel like I've known them for years. it didn't matter that my fish wasn't the best I've ever had. That my S'mores cake was absolutely awesome and now sitting on my thighs. That the check was $135. Our dinner was one of the best we've ever had, because my husband didn't listen to me. We had a party of six. And it was amazingly unforgettable.

We're all ready to leave, and the couple to my left, the younger one with the quiet husband, get ready to leave. She hands him his folded cane, which Jasen doesn't notice. He whips it into place, and my husband basically jumps into his new friend's lap.

"What the hell is that? What the hell are you gonna do with that?"

The wife chuckles "he's blind."

"Seriously, Jasen. Good lord." But the husband smiles sweetly. And say they love us.

They leave, and the couple beside us burst into laughter. The wife knew he was blind. The husband, no idea.

We picked up Juni, and both of my men were asleep before we hit the interstate. I drove home, smiling and listening to Enya. It was a perfect night. And worth every penny, because of my Redneck Husband.

Soup with the Redneck

As previously mentioned, the Redneck Husband is a phenomenal cook. He can pile what looks like a load of crap into a pot and onto the grill, and out comes a culinary masterpiece. Last night, it was soup made from leftovers. A delectable, refrigerator-cleaning bowl of yumminess.

Problem is, eating soup next to Jasen is anything but a masterpiece. Juni couldn't wait for dinner before his bath time, so it was just Jasen and I perched at the bar. At first, I felt elated that he scooted next to me. Usually, Juni plops down in the middle chair.

It began with the seasoning. Pepper so heavy it lofted my way and made my eyes water and burn, and sneeze. I'm estimating about 3/4 of the pepper actually made it into the bowl. The rest landed on the bar. Waiting for me to sponge it off. Lovely.

Then began the actual eating. I swear, it was like the man hadn't eaten in 32 days. Noodles slurped into his mouth, spewing chicken broth droplets on the side of my cheek. And of course on the bar, again, waiting for that sponge.

I'm quirky. I know this. One of those quirks happens to be hearing people eat. As a child and teenager, I couldn't eat cereal near my mom. She crunched too loud. Jasen brings an all new meaning to loud eating. He slurps. He sips. He moans and groans in gluttonous happiness. Makes me laugh and drives me crazy, all at the same time.

Later that night Juni passed out on the couch before his bedtime. I don't know what I was thinking, but I thought it would be nice to eat orange slices in bed with Jasen. Yeah...not so much. I thought eating soup was loud.

Tears of Joy

My husband may be a redneck, but he's a sensitive redneck. It's one of the reasons I love him. He cries over a good birthday card, a sad movie, and especially over the beauty in our son.

But tonight, Jasen surprised me. he cried at dinner not because Juni said "I love you Daddy" or I gave him a heartfelt card. He cried because Juni loved his baby back ribs.

That's right. My husband teared up because our son was gnawing on a pork rib like a tiger cub after its first kill.

Waffles, Bacon and a Rotten Egg

Sunday mornings are nothing short of glorious in our home. Juni plays trains while Jasen cooks breakfast, and I sleep an extra 15 minutes.

Jasen always concocts something amazing. This morning he presented Belgian apple waffles, bacon, omelets and a rotten egg.

The rotten egg put a serious damper on our morning.

Jasen and Juni pick the eggs. Occasionally, they forget one. Which is fine. As long as the egg isn't refrigerated, it won't go bad for quite a while.

Apparently, one of the eggs Jasen decided to put into his omelet somehow turned bad. Very bad. Green, actually. He cracked it open, and immediately began gagging. He threw it in the trash, and realized he needed to take the entire can outside to rid our kitchen of the rancid smell. Even that didn't work. He's running the dishwasher, with the omelet pan inside. Wiping the counters. And gagging. Every few minutes he darted out the porch door yelling he was going to puke.

All I could do was laugh. And hide. I've never smelled a rotten egg, and decided that it was completely possible for me to take one whiff and never eat another poultry produced protein morsel in my life.

I screamed at him to spray some air freshener. But of course he was too busy with omelet number two.

Jasen eradicated the kitchen of the green egg (feeding it to my now very gassy and smelly pup) and sat down to eat his omelet.

And smelled his fingers. Not good. He ran from the living room, gagging and diving for the sink. Three washes later, and he still dared me to sniff his pinkie. No way. One negative to having fresh eggs is, every now and then, there is bound to be a rotten one in the bunch. The rest of the carton is still sitting in our fridge, awaiting its fate. Apparently, the smell was so bad that Jasen can't decide if he wants to risk a nasal disaster again.

Feta Face

Our home is filled with smells. Candles, baking cookies in the winter, maybe a nice dinner in the crock pot.

And the smell of my boys. Of course by boys I mean my Redneck Husband and our son. My son refuses to wear socks with his new "big boy" shoes. He picked them out himself, and has decided it's a fashion statement to either wear just one sock, or none. I love the shoes. They're skater shoes with a skull and cross-bones on the toe. Very grown up. And so is the smell. Wearing no socks is not a good thing for a boy, apparently. We were driving in the car the other day when he kicked off his shoes. I seriously almost fainted. Jasen didn't even notice the smell, and I'm driving with my head out the window like the neighbor's dog.

I shouldn't have been shocked. He takes after his father. Not that my husband has stinky feet. In fact, he has the softest, best-smelling feet ever. It's just not fair that a man has such silky feet. But when he eats butter, it's a different story.

My husband could grow a full beard at age 14. I kid you not. I took him to my junior prom and people called him Grisly Adams. The man has hair on every inch of his body. Now he has a goatee.

Butter and goatees do not mix. When they do mix, it creates a smell just like that of feta cheese. I know this, because my husband gets what we call "feta face" after eating artichokes dipped in butter, buttered corn, lobster slobbered with butter - basically anything that would allow butter to get on his facial hair.

We coined the term a few years ago when we were newly married. He'd never tried artichokes, and I love them. We had a great night, and snuggled in on the couch for some kissy-face. And then we smelled it. I was scared it was me, he was scared it was him. We ignored it for a few minutes, but just couldn't stand it. Both of us blurted out in unison "What the fuck is that SMELL?" He smelled my hair, I smelled his shirt. We smelled everything around the couch. We couldn't figure it out. Until we kissed again. It was his goatee. His friggin goatee smelled like feta cheese.

To this day we have found no remedy for feta face. Dove, Pantene, rubbing alcohol. Nothing washes or strips the smell away.

And it's only real butter that does it. If we use a spread, feta face doesn't show himself. So no butter will ever find itself on an artichoke, corn or any other food that could cover his hair. And if my redneck husband does decide to indulge in that wonderful buttery dip, my lips are off limits. Feta Face is not someone I'm big on making out with.

Who Stole the Fucking Cookies?...

Jasen and Juni did the grocery shopping one week. I was just too much of a wreck after losing Shelby after I accidentally ran her over with my 4-Runner. They came back with three things: a 3 lb. bag of shredded mozzarella cheese, chocolate oatmeal cookie dough, and that frozen cookie dough that is already in the shape of cookies, so you can bake one or 12.

I love cookie dough. Especially sugar cookie dough. I could eat it at least 3 times a day. My husband knows this, and therefore never keeps it in the house. He knows I'd eat it and then blame him for bringing the evil substance into my home.

Jasen and Juni had cookies that night, and I will admit I had two. I also fully admit I ate a raw one just before bed. It was probably midnight or so. The next night, Juni asked for the sugar cookies, and Jasen couldn't find them. He asked me, I said I'd eaten one the night before, and that I'd also returned them to the freezer.

My redneck husband proceeded to tell me that cookies don't just walk away. Someone took them. And that someone was me. He actually accused me not only of eating 12 raw cookies, but then hiding the empty wrapper in the trash, and then lying about it. Are you kidding me? I pretty much shut down at that point. I could care less where the cookies were, and figured Juni had put them somewhere in a pretend kitchen. I was sure we'd find them by following either the smell or ants in a few weeks.

But my husband, at 8 p.m., actually went outside to the big trash can, and dug through it. Because he thought his wife would actually eat that much and hide the evidence. My feelings were definitely crushed, but beyond that I was just plain pissed. Thirty minutes and 55 arguments later Jasen found said cookie dough in the freezer; it had just fallen under the drawer.

I asked for an apology, and he refused. Said he still thinks it's something I would do. I don't think he realized why I'd been pretty much silent to him for three days. He goes through these phases where he'll just completely become agitated at me for no reason, and then ride my butt like ... well I don't even know what. He's in one of those phases where I'm supposed to cook dinner, cut the grass, do the paperwork for the business, run all the errands, clean the house, be where and do what he needs at a moment's notice and ... oh yeah ... raise a human being to be a positive addition to the human race. No biggie... I've totally got this under control...

My marriage is wonderful. We play, laugh, fight and repeat. The Redneck Husband is funny without knowing it, leading me to have a book of notes with his antics waiting for me to type them into history for all to read.

There's more to come from Stories from a Redneck's Wife. This is just the beginning, folks. Stay tuned for more.

Made in the USA
Lexington, KY
17 December 2017